THE TYRANNY OF GUILT

PASCAL BRUCKNER

Translated from the French by STEVEN RENDALL

The Tyranny of Guilt

An Essay on Western Masochism

PRINCETON UNIVERSITY PRESS

Princeton and Oxford

Published by Princeton University Press, 41 William Street, Princeton, New Jersey 08540
In the United Kingdom: Princeton University Press, 6 Oxford Street, Woodstock, Oxfordshire OX20 1TW

press.princeton.edu

Library of Congress Cataloging-in-Publication Data
Bruckner, Pascal.
   [Tyrannie de la pénitence. English]
   The tyranny of guilt: an essay on Western masochism / Pascal Bruckner; translated from the French by Steven Rendall.
     p. cm.
   Includes index.
   ISBN 978-0-691-14376-7 (cloth : alk. paper) 1. Civilization, Western—20th century. 2. Civilization, Western—21st century. 3. International relations—Moral and ethical aspects. 4. Western countries—Foreign relations. 5. Western countries—Intellectual life. 6. Guilt 7. Self-hate (Psychology) 8. World politics. I. Title.
   CB245.B7613 2010
   909'.09821--dc22   2009032666

British Library Cataloging-in-Publication Data is available

Cet ouvrage, publié dans le cadre d'un programme d'aide à la publication, bénéficie du soutien du Ministère des Affaires étrangères et du Service Culturel de l'Ambassade de France aux Etats-Unis.

This work, published as part of a program of aid for publication, received support from the French Ministry of Foreign Affairs and the Cultural Services of the French Embassy in the United States.

This book has been composed in Minion Pro
Printed on acid-free paper. ∞
Printed in the United States of America
10 9 8 7 6 5 4 3 2 1

JUN 01 2011 ⅅ

For Laurent Aublin, my oldest and most loyal friend, in memory of the dormitory at Henri-IV and the Dôme des Écrins

I've drunk too much of the black blood of the dead.

—MICHELET

We live in a time when men, driven by mediocre,

ferocious ideologies, are becoming used to being

ashamed of everything. Ashamed of themselves,

ashamed to be happy, to love and to create . . . .

So we have to feel guilty. We are being dragged

before the secular confessional, the worst of all.

—ALBERT CAMUS

   Actuelles. Écrits politiques, 1948

CONTENTS

INTRODUCTION   *1*

CHAPTER ONE

Guilt Peddlers   5

　The Irremediable and Despondency   6

　The Ideology That Stammers   9

　The Self-Flagellants of the Western World   13

　A Thirst for Punishment   22

CHAPTER TWO

The Pathologies of Debt   27

　Placing the Enemy in One's Heart   28

　The Vanities of Self-Hatred   33

　One-Way Repentance   40

　The False Quarrel over Islamophobia   47

CHAPTER THREE

Innocence Recovered   57

　How Central Is the Near East?   59

　"Zionism, the Criminal DNA of Humanity"   62

　Unmasking the Usurper   67

　A Delicate Arbitrage   74

　America Doubly Damned   80

CHAPTER FOUR

The Fanaticism of Modesty 87

   A Tardy Conversion to Virtue 88

   The Empire of Emptiness 90

   The Pacification of the Past 93

   The Guilty Imagination 96

   Recovering Self-Esteem 100

   The Twofold Lesson 106

CHAPTER FIVE

The Second Golgotha 111

   Misinterpretations of Auschwitz 113

   Hitlerizing History 117

   The Twofold Colonial Nostalgia 127

CHAPTER SIX

Listen to My Suffering 139

   On Victimization as a Career 140

   Protect Minorities or Emancipate the Individual? 148

   What Duty of Memory? 157

CHAPTER SEVEN

Depression in Paradise: France, a Symptom and Caricature of Europe 167

   A Universal Victim? 168

   The Wild Ass's Skin 176

   Who Are the Reactionaries? 179

   The Triumph of Fear 183

   Metamorphosis or Decline? 186

CHAPTER EIGHT
*Doubt and Faith: The Quarrel between Europe
and the United States*   193
   To Be or to Have   194
   The Troublemakers in History   199
   The Archaism of the Soldier   203
   The Swaggering Colossus   207

CONCLUSION   215

POSTSCRIPT TO THE ENGLISH TRANSLATION   223

INDEX   229

THE TYRANNY OF GUILT

A great city in northern Europe is struck by an unusual heat wave in the middle of winter as an asteroid approaches Earth. In the evening, residents go out into the streets in their pajamas, wiping away the sweat that is running down their cheeks, and look anxiously up at the sky, seeing the asteroid grow larger as they watch. They all fear the same thing: that this mass of molten matter will collide with our planet. Hordes of panicked rats are fleeing the sewers, car tires are exploding, the asphalt is melting. Then a strange figure dressed in a white sheet and wearing a long beard begins to harangue the crowd, striking a gong and shouting: "This is punishment, repent, the end of Time has come."

We smile at this tawdry prophet belching forth prophesies, since this scene occurs in a comic book, Hergé's *The Shooting Star*.[1] However, beneath the silliness, what truth there is in the cry: "Repent!" That is the message that, under cover of its proclaimed hedonism, Western philosophy

---

[1] Casterman, 1947.

has been hammering into us for the past half-century—
though that philosophy claims to be both an emancipa-
tory discourse and the guilty conscience of its time. What
it injects into us in the guise of atheism is nothing other
than the old notion of original sin, the ancient poison of
damnation. In Judeo-Christian lands, there is no fuel so
potent as the feeling of guilt, and the more our philosophers and sociologists proclaim themselves to be agnos-
tics, atheists, and free-thinkers, the more they take us back
to the religious belief they are challenging. As Nietzsche
put it, in the name of humanity secular ideologies have
out-Christianized Christianity and taken its message still
further.

From existentialism to deconstructionism, all of modern thought can be reduced to a mechanical denunciation
of the West, emphasizing the latter's hypocrisy, violence,
and abomination. In this enterprise the best minds have
lost much of their substance. Few of them have avoided
succumbing to this spiritual routine: one applauds a religious revolution, another goes into ecstasies over the
beauty of terrorist acts or supports a guerilla movement
because it challenges our imperialist project. Indulgence
toward foreign dictatorships, intransigence toward our
democracies. An eternal movement: critical thought, at
first subversive, turns against itself and becomes a new
conformism, but one that is sanctified by the memory of
its former rebellion. Yesterday's audacity is transformed
into clichés. Remorse has ceased to be connected with
precise historical circumstances; it has become a dogma, a

spiritual commodity, almost a form of currency. A whole intellectual intercourse is established: clerks are appointed to maintain it like the ancient guardians of the sacred flame and issue permits to think and speak. At the slightest deviation, these athletes of contrition protest, enforce proper order in language, accord their imprimatur or refuse it. In the great factory of the mind, it is they who open doors for you or slam them in your face. This repeated use of the scalpel against ourselves we call the duty of repentance. Like any ideology, this discourse is at first presented in the register of the obvious. There is no need for demonstrations because things seem clear: one has only to repeat and confirm. The duty to repent is a multifunction fighting machine: it censures, reassures, and distinguishes.

First of all, the duty to repent forbids the Western bloc, which is eternally guilty, to judge or combat other systems, other states, other religions. Our past crimes command us to keep our mouths closed. Our only right is to remain silent. Next, it offers those who repent the comfort of redemption. Reserve and neutrality will redeem us. No longer participating, no longer getting involved in the affairs of our time, except perhaps by approving of those whom we formerly oppressed. In this way, two different Wests will be defined: the good one, that of the old Europe that withdraws and keeps quiet, and the bad one, that of the United States that intervenes and meddles in everything.

Of course, one cannot train whole generations to practice self-flagellation without paying a price. There are negative effects associated with certain secondary benefits. A movement I described in 1983[2] is now spreading and growing deeper. But we are no longer in the age of the white man's tears, an ephemeral prostration of the former dominator before those who were his slaves when the Cold War and the still lively hope for a worldwide revolution galvanized a continent whose eastern portion had been colonized by the USSR. The Old World, which has fallen victim to its victory over communism, has laid down its arms since the fall of the Berlin Wall. An atmosphere of renunciation has replaced the euphoria of triumph. Africa, Asia, the Near East, the whole world is knocking at the door of Europe, wants to gain a foothold in it at the time when it is wallowing in shame and self-loathing. This book seeks to understand this paradox, to define our moral decay, and to offer some theoretical tools to remedy it.

[2] In *Le Sanglot de l'homme blanc: Tiers-Monde, culpabilité, haine de soi* (Paris: Seuil, 1983). English translation: *The Tears of the White Man: Compassion as Contempt* (New York: Free Press, 1986).

CHAPTER ONE
Guilt Peddlers

Everyone is guilty with respect to everyone else,

for everything, and I more than anyone.

—FYODOR DOSTOYEVSKY

The Irremediable and Despondency

The whole world hates us, and we deserve it: that is what most Europeans think, at least in Western Europe. Since 1945 our continent has been obsessed by torments of repentance. Ruminating on its past abominations—wars, religious persecutions, slavery, imperialism, fascism, communism—it views its history as nothing more than a long series of massacres and sackings that led to two world wars, that is, to an enthusiastic suicide. Unparalleled horrors, the industrialization of death on a grand scale in the Nazi and Soviet camps, the promotion of bloodthirsty clowns to the rank of mass idols, and the experience of radical evil transformed into bureaucratic routine: that is what we have achieved. And the greatest virtues—work, order, discipline—have been put to the most dreadful ends, science has been dishonored, culture mocked in all its pretensions, idealism disfigured. Europe, like a groggy boxer stunned by the blows he has absorbed, feels overcome by crimes that are too heavy to bear. There is no nation in the west or east of this little continental peninsula that does not have to examine its conscience, and whose history is not full of corpses, guard towers, tortures, and exactions. So many sublime works, lofty metaphysics, and subtle philosophies, all just to end up in civil wars, charnel houses, gas chambers, the Gulag. Europe has combined, in an unparalleled way, calculating thought with murder, constructing methodically and systematically a dehumanizing machine that reached its apogee in the twentieth century. A curse is hidden behind our civilization that corrupts its meaning and mocks its grandeur. The highpoints of thought, music, art—all that useless and tragic luxury has as its corollary abysses of abjection.

In 1955, when Claude Lévi-Strauss discussed the Indians of Brazil in his *Tristes Tropiques*, he noted with consternation "the monstrous and incomprehensible cataclysm represented, for such a broad and innocent part of humanity, by the development of Western civilization."[1] Today, countless travelers and theoreticians continue to bear witness to this feeling of repulsion. Forty years after Lévi-Strauss wrote these lines, the same view continues to be expressed: "Collectively, we have many faults that need to be pardoned," the philosopher Jean-Marc Ferry observes. "We have to remember, in a critical way, the violence and humiliation we have inflicted on whole peoples on every continent in order to impose our own vision of humanity and civilization."[2] A historian specializing in Algeria writes with dismay that "the French have never seen guilt as a constitutive part of their history."[3] In a series of lectures delivered in 2005, Edgar Morin sees in a pacified Europe, and in it alone, the ferment of a potential barbarity: "We have to be capable of conceiving European barbarity in order to transcend it, because the worst is still possible. Amid the threatening wasteland of barbarity, we are for the moment in a relatively protected oasis. But we also know that we are living in historical, political, and

---

[1] Claude Lévi-Strauss, *Tristes Tropiques* (Paris: Plon, 1955), p. 375.

[2] Jean-Marc Ferry, *Les Puissances de l'expérience: essai sur l'identité contemporaine*, 2 vols. (Paris: Le Cerf, 1991), p. 219.

[3] Benjamin Stora, "Les Aveux les plus durs," in Patrick Weil and Stéphane Dufoix, *L'Esclavage, la colonialisation et après* (Paris: PUF, 2005), p. 591.

social conditions that make the worst conceivable, particularly in moments of paroxysm."[4]

All Europeans should be convinced that Europe is the sick man of the planet, which it is infecting with its pestilence. To the question, "Who is to blame?" in the metaphysical sense of the term, the standard, spontaneous response is: "We are." The West, that alliance between the Old and the New Worlds, is a machine without a soul or a captain that has put "humanity in its service." Henceforth it lives in the age of the "revenge of the Crusaders" [sic] and seeks to export its "unbridled passions" everywhere.[5] There is no monstrosity in Africa, Asia, or the Near East for which it is not to blame:

> The Third World is the outlet for passions unleashed by the chaotic play of uncontrolled competitions. At the origin of the mad bloodbaths in the Third World that spread horror in humble shacks and confirm us in the belief that the Other is a barbarian, we find the frustrations created by the West. Examples are legion: peaceful Cambodia plunged into an unprecedented genocide following American intervention, Iran deprived of Mossadegh's bourgeois revolution by Anglo-American intervention, and the blind terrorism of the kidnappings, hijackings, and hostage-taking elicited by the nightmare of the Middle East.[6]

[4] Edgar Morin, *Culture et barbarie européennes* (Paris: Bayard, 2005), p. 92.
[5] Serge Latouche, *L'Occidentalisation du monde* (Paris: La Découverte, 1992; new ed., 2005), pp. 26, 27.
[6] Ibid., p. 77.

Extermination is "at the heart of European thought" (Sven Lindqvist), and its imperialism is "a biologically necessary process that leads, in accord with natural laws, to the inevitable elimination of inferior races."[7] If the West "was probably able to produce computers only because somewhere people were dying of hunger and desires,"[8] the conclusion to be drawn is obvious: we have to resist its disintegrating power by all means at our disposal.

The Ideology That Stammers

Europe against itself: anti-Occidentalism, as we know, is a European tradition that stretches from Montaigne to Sartre and instills relativism and doubt in a serene conscience sure that it is in the right. In the time of Las Casas, it took a certain audacity to denounce the barbarity of the conquistadors or the civilizing mission of the great powers during the period of empires. Nowadays all it takes to attack Europe is a bit of conformism. Thus, in 1925, in the middle of the war in the Moroccan Rif waged by Abd el-Krim's rebel tribes against French and Spanish troops, Louis Aragon, then twenty-eight years old, gave a talk in Madrid before an audience of students that was as magnificent as it was crazy, vibrating with fury:

---

[7] Sven Lindqvist, *Exterminez toutes ces brutes. L'odyssée d'un homme au coeur de la nuit et les origines du génocide européen* (Paris: Le Serpent à plumes, 1998). Original in Swedish (1992). Quoted in Géraldine Faes and Stephen Smith, *Noir et français* (Paris: Panama, 2006), pp. 324–25.

[8] Latouche, *L'Occidentalisation du monde*, p. 120.

We will overcome everything. And first of all we will destroy this civilization that you cherish, in which you are cast like fossils in schist.

Western world, you are condemned to death. We are the defeatists of Europe. . . . Let the Orient, your terror, finally answer your voice. We will awaken everywhere the germs of confusion and malaise. We are the agitators of the mind.

All barricades are good, all obstacles to our happiness are bad. Jews, come out of the ghettos. Let the people go hungry so that it finally experiences the taste of bread and anger. Move, thousand-armed India, great legendary Brahma. It's your turn, Egypt! And let drug dealers attack our terrified countries. . . . Arise, world! See how this earth is dry and good for all kinds of bonfires. You'd think it was straw.

Go ahead, laugh. We are those who will always hold out our hands to the enemy.[9]

Eighty years later the same idea is formulated insipidly, like a bailiff's report: delighted that resistance to our enterprise is sprouting up everywhere, the economist and philosopher Serge Latouche asserts that "the death of the West will not necessarily be the end of the world" but, on the contrary, "the condition for the blossoming of new worlds, of a new civilization, a new era."[10] In the meantime, challenge has deteriorated into an automatism, and

---

[9] *La Révolution surréaliste*, no. 4, quoted in André Rezler, *L'Intellectuel contre l'Europe* (Paris: PUF, 1976), p. 81.
[10] Latouche, *L'Occidentalisation du monde*, p. 158.

destructive jubilance has bogged down in frigid bureaucratic language.

In this regard, one cannot help having a strange feeling
that we are witnessing a remake, as if the old saws from the
1960s were coming back to haunt us. But that overlooks a
fundamental point: just as the communist idea is becoming seductive again as the memory of the Soviet Union
becomes fainter, Third Worldism is flourishing again as
Maoism, the Khmer Rouge, and the South American gue-
rillas are forgotten. It is precisely the failure of these concrete utopias that explains the resurgence of the doctrine,
which has suddenly been freed from the need to corre-
spond to reality. Ideologies never die, they metamorphose
and are reborn in a new form just when they are thought
buried forever: failure, far from serving as a drying-out
cell, relaunches the drunkenness. The suffering face of the
colonized person has been replaced by the suffering face
of the decolonized person who over the past forty years
has passed through a series of disenchantments and fias-
cos: the Great Helmsman and his seventy million dead,
Pol Pot's general massacres, Vietnamese repression and
the exodus of the boat people, Saddam Hussein's dictatorship, the obscurantist madness of the Iranian mullahs,
Cuban fascism, the Algerian civil war, the disarray of the
various tropical socialist regimes, without mentioning
corruption, impoverishment, waste, and nepotism.

For half a century, the heart of darkness has no longer
been the epic of colonialism. It is independent Africa, "that
cocktail of disasters," as Kofi Annan modestly called it in
2001: the murderous reign of the Red Negus, Mengistu;

the macabre buffoonery of an Idi Amin, Sekou Touré, or Bokassa; the madness of a Samuel Doe or a Charles Taylor in Liberia; in Sierra Leone, the blood diamonds of a Foday Sankho, who invented "short-sleeve" mutilation by cutting people's arms off at the elbow, and "long-sleeve" mutilation by cutting their arms off at the shoulder; the use of child soldiers, killer kids who are beaten and drugged; detention camps; mass rapes; the endless conflict between Ethiopia and Eritrea; the civil wars in Chad, Sudan, Somalia, Uganda, and Côte d'Ivoire; cannibalism in the Congo; crimes against humanity in Darfur; and, last but not least, the genocide in Rwanda and the Great Lakes war, with its three to four million victims since 1998. Decolonization was a great process of democratic equality: the former slaves achieved within a few years the same level of bestiality as their former masters. The only remarkable exceptions to this somber account are South Africa and Botswana, the small and large dragons of Asia, and the irruption of India and China, both of which have gone over to capitalism in a revenge taken by the thieves of fire on the earlier dominators.

What did the crowd of young people shout to Jacques Chirac in 2004, during the first visit by a French president to Algeria since decolonization? "Visas, visas." A malicious wit might say: they drove us out and now they all want to come live with us! That does not cast doubt on the legitimacy of their independence, but it does explain this disturbing truth: Europe got over the loss of its colonies much more quickly than the colonies got over their loss of Europe. Since the latter has not sunk body and soul in the convulsions of decolonization, giving the lie to those who connected its wealth with the pillaging of the Southern Hemisphere and unequal trade, all that remains is constantly to insist on its perversity. The globe henceforth constituting, thanks to the media, a glass house in which everyone is more or less aware of everyone else's condition, the disease of comparison accelerates the competition among peoples. The old dream of salvation by proletarian nations was temporarily suspended (even if we see it reconstituting itself in South America on an anti-imperialist front led by Venezuelan president Hugo Chávez), there is a return to the rhetoric of recrimination, especially since the worldwide offensive of Islam, and the disarray of many immigrants lends this discourse a new legitimacy—a curious example of a Third Worldism that survived the disappearance of the Third World as an autonomous entity. The former, which evaporated in the 1980s, was a Third Worldism of projection, supporting regimes thought to incarnate the new revolutionary Eden. Its current avatar is a Third Worldism of introspection, turned against itself: we hate ourselves much more than we love others. The malaise, ceasing to be supported by a political project, gnaws away at Western consciousness from within. A change in scale, a narrowing of horizons.

The Self-Flagellants of the Western World

In 1947 Maurice Merleau-Ponty, still a communist fellow-traveler, tried to understand the logic of the Moscow purge trials that ten years earlier had led Stalin to eliminate his former companions, who had been renamed "enemies of the people."[11] Even if they were innocent of the charges brought against them, these hard-core Bolsheviks confessed their sins, accusing themselves of imaginary crimes. They invented all kinds of betrayals of the proletariat and died with full confidence in the future of the revolution. Relatively speaking, the mentality of accusation still subsists in our reflex to spontaneously blame ourselves for the planet's ills. The average European, whether male or female, is extremely sensitive, always ready to shoulder the blame for the poverty of Africa or Asia, to sorrow over the world's problems, to assume responsibility for them, always ready to ask what Europeans can do for the South rather than asking what the South could do for itself.

By the evening of September 11, 2001, many Europeans, despite their obvious sympathy for the victims, were telling themselves that the Americans deserved what they got. The cream of the European intelligentsia immediately adopted that line with an abundance of rhetorical subtleties: the hijackers who had destroyed the World Trade Center towers were only the agents of a ruthless punishment. We saw two-bit Neros applauding this double attack and finding in it the execution of an immanent justice. Tit for tat, the re-establishment of a balance upset by an excessive dissymmetry—that was the interpretation offered by Jean Baudrillard in an utterly religious justification of this vengeance:

[11] Maurice Merleau-Ponty, *Humanisme et terreur*, introduction by Claude Lefort (Paris: NRF/Gallimard, 1980).

When the situation is monopolized in this way by the world power, when one has to deal with this enormous condensation of all functions by technocratic machinery and the dominant way of thinking, how can one proceed except by a terrorist transfer of the situation? It is the system itself that has created the objective conditions of this brutal retaliation. By taking all the cards into its own hand, it forces the Other to change the rules of the game . . . terror against terror, there is no longer any ideology behind all that.

But the terrorist attacks on March 11, 2004, in Madrid (200 dead) proved that Europeans had also internalized the crime: the decision of Zapatero's new left-wing government to withdraw Spanish troops from Iraq (fulfilling a previous commitment) made it seem that he was yielding to the demands of the bombers and that the carnage in the Atocha train station was caused by Madrid's involvement, in alliance with Washington, in the second Gulf War (whereas terrorist cells continued their attacks long after the withdrawal, arguing that the Muslims lost Andalusia in the fifteenth century). Let us recall that in Madrid a million citizens protested, with not a single cry of hatred against Arabs, limiting themselves to booing José Aznar, who had drawn them into Iraq against their will and had wrongly accused the Basque separatist organization ETA of having planted the bombs. Today the massacre is still attributed to the leader of the populist Right, who has been elevated to the status of a convenient scapegoat, which makes it possible to avoid looking into the real causes. The bombs that exploded in London on July 7, 2005, killing almost sixty people, have also given rise to a whole rhetoric of expiation. The following day, the headline in *Le Parisien*, which is not particularly known for being left-wing, read: "Al-Qaeda Punishes London" (the paper later apologized for using this phrase). The mayor of London, Ken Livingstone, a committed Leftist known for his hostility to Israel, condemned the attacks but soon afterward explained that the Arab countries have to be left alone, perhaps forgetting that most of the terrorists were British subjects of Pakistani origin:

> The suicide attacks would probably not have happened had Western powers left Arab nations free to decide their own affairs after World War I. I think you've just had 80 years of Western intervention into predominantly Arab lands because of the Western need for oil. . . . If at the end of the First World War we had done what we promised the Arabs, which was to let them be free and have their own governments, and kept out of Arab affairs, and just bought their oil, rather than feeling we had to control the flow of oil, I suspect this wouldn't have arisen.[12]

Reversing the burden of proof, making civilians torn apart by steel and fire guilty in spite of themselves, is what the British writer John Le Carré also achieves. Regretting that in Great Britain, as in the United States, there is in

[12] *Le Monde*, July 21, 2005.

practice "no parliamentary opposition" [*sic*], he sees the sources of terrorism in frustrations and humiliations, both past and present:

> When communities have been exploited for a long time, this creates in them a desire for revenge, no matter how psychotic or mistaken it may be. To understand what produces this psychosis that leads people to want to "kill, kill, kill," it suffices to observe these communities.[13]

A French sociologist, Farhad Khosrokhavar, explains the attacks as the result of the humiliation of the Arab-Muslim world in general "because of the creation of Israel, because of the feeling that Islam has become the religion of the oppressed."[14] Interviewed by the French Press Agency on July 13, 2005, another sociologist, François Burgat, confirms this analysis: without the impression of injustice felt by the Arab masses with regard to the Israel-Palestinian conflict and the perception of a double standard in the way Israel and Iraq are treated politically, such events would never have occurred.

It is clear that if tomorrow terrorists should blow up the Parisian Metro, topple the Eiffel Tower, or destroy Notre Dame, we would hear the same argument. Sensitive people on both the Left and the Right would urge us to blame ourselves: we have been attacked, so we are guilty, whereas our attackers are in reality poor wretches protesting against our insolent wealth, our way of life, our

[13] Ibid.
[14] *Le Monde*, July 17, 2005.

predatory economy. Spontaneously, our judgment of ourselves grants that our adversaries are right. After each explosion, there is a flood of panicked efforts to explain it
that invokes all the problems of the world simultaneously,
so eager are we to put our motivations into the mouths
of the jihadists, even if we disapprove of their methods.
And to counteract their terrifying silence, we speak for
them, we tell them what to say. "Who are our enemies?"
Dominique de Villepin asks. "The world's wounds are
many. Out of habit, weakness, fear, it is tempting to mix
everything up in a stubborn struggle against a diabolical
adversary."[15] But we don't choose our enemies in accord
with our wishes or our convictions; it is they who des-
ignate us as enemies, strike us when they wish, and seek
our destruction. Whence the feeling of a certain schizophrenia in old Europe: alongside the United States, we are
fighting a terrorism whose importance we never cease to
deny or minimize. For some, this constitutes a kind of "intellectual fraud" that will put us under Washington's control.[16] For others, such as the Spanish prime minister José
Luis Zapatero, we have to push euphemism to the point
of refusing to name the danger: "I never speak of Islamist
terrorism, but only of international terrorism. We cannot
lump together under one name hundreds of millions of
people and a religion that, like all religions in the history
of humanity, includes an element of religious fanaticism."[17]
Entirely committed to denial, our leaders thus ask Europe

[15] Dominique de Villepin, *Le Requin et la Mouette* (Paris: Plon, 2004), p. 113.
[16] Pascal Boniface, *Le Nouvel Observateur*, December 18, 2005.
[17] Interview in *Le Monde*, June 29, 2004.

to attack the roots of the problem, which are "injustice, resentment, and frustration" (Dominique de Villepin). It is not a matter of fighting but rather of "trying to understand" the other, because "knowing is fundamental" and "the use of force leads nowhere" (Mario Soares).

But these interpretive schemes suffer from a major problem: they confuse pretexts with causes. It is true that when existing pathologies find no outlet, terrorism grafts itself onto them and overdetermines them. However, its ultimate motivation is fanatics' hostility to the principle of an open society in which formal equality is recognized for everyone. It is our existence as such that is intolerable for them. But this observation is intolerable for us: in order to remain within the bounds of reason and to nourish the idea that "even the enemies of reason . . . must be, in some fashion, reasonable" (Paul Berman), we must at all costs provide arguments for the killers, even if in doing so we seem to justify their acts.

Just as there are those within radical Islamism who preach hate, so there are preachers of hate within our democracies, especially among the intellectual elites, and their proselytizing is no less intense. To hear them tell it, we are far from being innocent because we allow, through a simple effect of power relationships, hunger, AIDS, inadequate medical care to exist. Speaking of September 11, Jacques Derrida explained:

> Does terrorism necessarily involve death? Can't one terrorize without killing? And then is killing necessarily something active? Can't "letting people

die" not wanting to know that one is letting people
die (hundreds of millions of people dying of hunger, AIDS, inadequate health care, etc.) be part of
a "more or less" conscious and deliberate terrorist
strategy? We are wrong to suppose too easily that
all terrorism is voluntary, conscious, organized, deliberate, intentionally calculated: there are historical
or political situations in which terror operates, so
to speak, by itself, through the simple effect of an
apparatus, through established power relationships,
without anyone, any conscious subject, any person,
being consciously aware of it or taking responsibility
for it. All situations of structural social or national
oppression produce a terror that is never natural
(and which is therefore organized, institutional)
and on which they depend without those who benefit from them ever having to organize terrorist acts
or be called terrorists.[18]

You've read that correctly: we're all potential terrorists;
to one degree or another, we sow death the way Monsieur
Jourdain spoke prose, without knowing it! To be sure, after finishing his implacable argument, Derrida ended up
declaring his preference for democracy. Nonetheless, by
revealing our manifold unconscious complicity with horror, he has proven that crime is our most widely shared
characteristic. Moreover, certain films have popularized
the image of those decent families, those peaceful little

[18] Giovanna Borradori, *Le Concept du 11 septembre. Dialogues avec Jacques
Derrida et Jürgen Habermas* (Paris: Galilée, 2004), pp. 162–63.

towns, that hide a terrible secret, an evil being. Suspicion gnaws at our most idyllic landscapes. Where we think we see an opposition with the fundamentalists, we must recognize an equivalence. Instead of being stupidly scandalized by explosions, let us begin by questioning ourselves, dissecting ourselves without respecting any taboo. Haven't we, after all, been asking for it, in a way? Beneath the appearance of a complex analysis, we find here the typical evangelical posture: self-accusation, public castigation. As good heirs of the Bible, we think that a great misfortune necessarily follows a great infraction. In this respect the intellectual caste, in our world, is the penitential class par excellence, continuing the role of the clergy under the Old Regime. We have to call its members what they are: officials of original sin. Obsessed with their desire to dismantle appearances, they never cease to insist on our naïveté. You think there's a radical opposition between the United States and Al-Qaeda? How childish—they're accomplices. What is terrorism, after all? A simple settling of accounts between rogue states, including America, since there's no real difference between them:

> There seems to be a powerful rationalization going on, consciously or unconsciously calculated. It consists in accusing and campaigning against so-called Rogue States, which in fact care little about international law. This rationalization is maneuvered by hegemonic states, starting with the United States, which was early and properly shown (Chomsky was not the only one to do so) to have long behaved as

"Rogue States." Moreover, every sovereign state is virtually and a priori capable of abusing its power and transgressing international law just like a Rogue State. There is a rogue element in every state.[19]

A Thirst for Punishment

Poor Europe: today as before, a stench of carrion rises from it, its past adheres to its present like a leprous mold. Whatever it does turns back on it in the form of a symptom of its disease. Take, for example, the waiting zones where foreigners without papers and asylum seekers are held. These are certainly not comparable to Nazi camps. Within our democratic societies they nonetheless share certain basic traits that define the paradigm of the concentration camp, that is, according to Giorgio Agamben, "a space that opens when the exception starts to become the rule. . . . they are places not governed by law."[20] After that, how can we be surprised when we are struck by heaven's thunderbolt, the wrath of Allah's madmen? How can we dare to judge the various barbarities that are ravaging humanity, when we have shown an "unparalleled savagery" in history?[21] We are paying for an ancient stain, we

[19] Jacques Derrida, *Voyous* (Paris: Galilée, 2003), pp. 214–15.
[20] Enzo Traverso, *Le passé, modes d'emploi* (Paris: La Fabrique, 2005), p. 84.
[21] Mariella Villasante Cervello, "La Négritude: une forme de racisme héritée de la colonisation française?" in Marc Ferro, *Le livre noir du colonialisme, XVIe–XXe siècle: de l'exterminaton à la repentance* (Paris: Hachette, 2004), p. 1018.

are retroactively responsible for the horrors committed by our ancestors or by other people. We can well say with the Psalmist: "O God, cleanse me of sins I do not perceive and forgive me those of others." Once again, let us admire the talent with which guilt is re-created, reinvented by the class of philosophers. We Europeans are born with a burden of vices and ugliness that mark us like stigmata, for we have to recognize that the white man has sown grief and ruin wherever he has gone. *For him, to exist is first of all to excuse himself.* Ferocity is white, as a lawyer of Colombian origin, Rosa Amelia Plumelle-Uribe, puts it in the title of her book, white and not black or red: the white man is genetically determined to kill, massacre, rape; he has split himself off from the rest of humanity in order to enslave it. He can't help it. His skin color is not only a matter of pigmentation but a moral defect, an inexpiable stain, as Professor Louis Sala-Molins explains in the preface to Plumelle-Uribe's work. He denounces the "wheeling-dealing voraciousness . . . of the white-American nations of Christianity" and sees every white venture as "an uninterrupted spiral of horror."[22]

What is the West, after all? The very figure of Satan, whose evil presence corrupts everything because it "has its center everywhere and its circumference nowhere" and occupies the head "of a warrior in Papua, a loin-cloth seller in Cotonou, and an imam in Qom" as well as that of

---

[22] Rosa Amelia Plumelle-Uribe, *La Férocité blanche, des non-Blancs aux non-Aryens, ces génocides occultés de 1492 à nos jours* (Paris: Albin Michel, 2001), preface by Louis Sala-Molins, pp. 9ff.

a speculator on the London Stock Exchange or a worker in the Renault factory.[23] Moreover, anyone who speaks up for it is not respectable (*fréquentable*).[24] It is a dizzying panorama: using the West as an explanation makes it possible to account for the totality of the real. The Euro-American is simultaneously cursed and indispensable: thanks to him, everything becomes clear, evil acquires a face, the dirty rat is universally designated. Biological, political, metaphysical guilt. And since we no longer believe in the kingdom of salvation, since Asia, Africa, and Latin America have (temporarily) ceased to be lands of redemption, nothing remains for us but to continue the execration ad nauseam.

[23] Latouche, *L'Occidentalisation du monde*, pp. 84–85.

[24] According to a professor in Quebec interviewed by Antoine Robitaille, "For some people, saying that one is a Westerner, acknowledging a kind of pride in belonging to that group, is practically equivalent to admitting that one is a criminal. It is to participate in a civilization that not long ago still thought it *was* the civilization, which colonized other peoples, ran a slave trade, and today . . . prospers as the result of an absolutely inequitable trade and, in addition, its way of life is leading toward an ecological apocalypse." Antoine Robitaille, "Le Choc des cultures, Peut-on se dire occidental et fier de l'être?" *Le Devoir* (Montreal), May 26, 2006.

Islamo-Leftism or Mutual Deception

"Today, confronted by the threat to Civilization, there is a response: revolutionary Islam! Only men and women armed with a total faith in the founding values of truth, justice, and fraternity will be prepared to lead the combat and deliver humanity from the empire of mendacity."[25] These remarks by the terrorist Carlos illustrate one of the most astonishing phenomena of recent years: the fusion between the atheist far Left and religious radicalism. In 1982 the Iranian philosopher Daryus Shayegan provided the best theoretical account of the collision between historical reason and atemporal revolution, "the ideologization of tradition," the overlapping of two incompatible orders such as we find it incarnated in the twentieth-century Shiite thinker Ali Shariati, who imposes Marxist categories on a prophetic cycle, working in spite of himself toward a secularization of Islam.[26] Islamo-Leftism was conceived chiefly by the British Trotskyites of the Socialist Workers' Party: noting that the religion of the Prophet, although reactionary, is a factor of upheaval and not of passivity at the heart of our societies, they promote a reasonable *entrisme*, tactical, temporary alliances with Islam.[27] A certain revolutionary fringe's hope that Islam might become the spearhead of a new insurrection in the name of the oppressed is not without ulterior motives on both sides: Trotskyites, supporters of alternative forms of

---

[25] Ilich Ramirez Sánchez, a.k.a. Carlos, L'Islam révolutionnaire (Paris: Editions du Rocher, 2003), p. 15.

[26] Daryus Shayegan, *Qu'est-ce qu'une révolution religieuse?* (Paris: Albin Michel, 1982; new ed. with new preface, 1991).

[27] Entrism is an old tactic used by communists and especially Trotskyites to infiltrate workers' or owners' organizations and gradually influence them.

globalism, and adherents to Third Worldism are using the Islamists as a battering ram against free-market capitalism. The hatred of the market is worth a few compromises regarding fundamental rights, and especially that of the equality between men and women. The fundamentalists, disguised as friends of tolerance, are dissimulating and using the Left to advance their interests under the mask of a progressive rhetoric. There is a twofold deception here: one side supports the Islamic veil or polygamy in the name of the struggle against racism and neocolonialism. The other side pretends to be attacking globalization in order to impose its version of religious faith. Two currents of thought form temporary alliances against a common enemy: it is not hard to predict which one will crush the other once its objectives have been achieved. The Leftist intransigence that refuses any compromise with bourgeois society and cannot castigate too severely "little white men" actively collaborates with the most reactionary elements in the Muslim religion. But if the far Left courts this totalitarian theocracy so assiduously, it is perhaps less a matter of opportunism than of a real affinity. The far Left has never gotten over communism and once again demonstrates that its true passion is not freedom, but slavery in the name of justice.

CHAPTER TWO

The Pathologies of Debt

He has lost all hope of Paradise, but he clings
to the wider hope of eternal damnation.

—VIRGINIA WOOLF

Europe of the Empires is now dying, and
it is the death agony of a pitiful princess.

—LÉOPOLD SÉDAR SENGHOR, 1960

A French teacher living in Libya, shocked by the caricatures of Muhammad that appeared during the winter of
2006 and noting the havoc they had wrought among his
students, wrote to the Paris newspaper *Le Monde* to express his indignation, concluding with these words: "We
are still the masters of the world and we seem to have
forgotten the sensitivities of those who aren't."[1] We are
masters of the world! Coming from a Disraeli or a Jules
Ferry, that expression wouldn't be surprising. But today,
in a left-wing newspaper, what presumption! We will see
that, paradoxically, this will to power is nourished by an
inextinguishable contrition.

Placing the Enemy in One's Heart

There is no doubt that Europe has given birth to monsters,
but at the same time it has given birth to theories that make it
possible to understand and destroy these monsters. Because
it has raised the alliance between progress and cruelty, between technological power and aggressiveness, to its highest point since the Conquistadors, because it has engaged
for centuries in bloody saturnalia, it has also developed an
acute sensibility to the follies of the human species. Taking
over from Arabs and Africans, it instituted the transatlantic
slave trade, but it also engendered abolitionism and put an
end to slavery before other nations did. It has committed the

---

[1] Robert Solé, *Le Monde*, "Courrier du médiateur," February 19–20, 2006.

worst crimes and has given itself the means of eradicating them. The peculiarity of Europe is a paradox pushed to the extreme: out of the medieval order came the Renaissance; out of feudalism, the aspiration to democracy; and out of the church's repression, the rise of the Enlightenment. The religious wars promoted secularism, national antagonisms promoted the hope of a supranational community, and the revolutions of the twentieth century promoted the antitotalitarian movement. Europe, like a jailer who throws you into prison and slips you the keys to your cell, brought into the world both despotism and liberty. It sent soldiers, merchants, and missionaries to subjugate and exploit distant lands,[2] but it also invented an anthropology that provides a way of seeing oneself from the other's point of view, of seeing the other in oneself, and oneself in the other—in short, of separating oneself from what is near in order to come closer to that from which one is separated.

For instance, the French Republic has committed abominations. It was also thanks to the Republic that we finally emerged from them when, after terrible convulsions, it finally brought its actions into accord with its principles. The colonial venture died from a double contradiction: it inflicted our particular customs on distant peoples on the

---

[2] Contrary to an image that has too long remained widespread, missionaries were not at all the government's obliging auxiliaries. The relation between religious missionary work and the interests of the mother country was a stormy one. Hence the important role played by the churches in decolonization, except in Portugal, where the concordat of May 7, 1940, put Catholic missions under the control of the state. See Marcel Merle, "L'anticolonialisme," in Ferro, *Le Livre noir du colonialisme*, pp. 815ff.

pretext that they were universal. Forcing pastis and ba-
guettes on Africans or pudding on Hindus was using trib-
alism to practice imperialism. Finally, by subjecting entire
continents to the laws of an imperial master and at the
same time inculcating in them the idea of nationalism and
the right to self-determination, the British, French, and
Dutch gave those whom they dominated the instruments
of their emancipation. In demanding their independence,
colonized peoples simply turned against their masters
the rules the latter had taught them, providing them in
spite of themselves with the weapons they needed to drive
the colonizers out. For example, it was in the name of the
rights of man and the citizen that the slaves in Haiti and
Santo Domingo revolted in the late eighteenth century,
discussing "the foundations of a new social contract on
the basis of the abolition of slavery, the equality of color,
and the destruction of colonial society."[3] And in 1954 the
nine historical leaders of the Algerian *Front de libération
nationale* had all been educated in French schools, where
they were taught the revolutionary ideals that were to incite them to rise up against Paris.

Here we have to distinguish colonialism, which is for
us, as moderns, fundamentally reprehensible, like fascism
and communism, from colonization, which was diverse
and complex, simultaneously harmful and beneficial, and
whose chronicling requires the scrupulous work of historians who respect facts and nuances. Colonization has not

[3] Florence Gauthier, quoted by Michel Giraud in Weil and Dufoix,
L'Esclavage, p. 538.

in every case prevented the weaving of ties or the mainte-
nance of friendly and respectful relations half a century
after its liquidation. As French living two thousand years
later, we can state that the Roman invasion of Gaul was
ultimately a good thing, and that without Caesar's defeat
of Vercingetorix at Alesia, without the infusion of Greco-
Roman culture into our territory, we would have long
remained a myriad of tribes with uncouth customs and
obscure forms of worship. Similarly, the Arab tutelage of
Spain up to the fifteenth century allowed the blossoming
of an extraordinary civilization, and the Ottoman Empire
itself would not have lasted such a long time had it not
represented, in certain respects, an authentic progress.
Nonetheless, in all these cases, nations rose up against this
foreign domination and destroyed it.[4] Under colonialism,
the occupied peoples are infantilized, belittled, and humiliated, while the occupying powers lose their souls, trample
on their own principles, and undergo a corruption of their
substance. Today we are stupefied by colonial writings jus-
tifying the elevation of "inferior races by superior races"
(Jules Ferry), and we find crazy the obstinacy of a certain
part of the Left under the Fourth Republic (Guy Mollet,
François Mitterand, Robert Lacoste) that wanted to keep

---

[4] We are too prone to forget that conquest and expansionism are not
peculiar to Europe. All great civilizations—Persians, Mongols, Chinese,
Aztecs, Incas—were colonizers. Muslims invaded Persia, India, Southeast
Asia, Sudan, and Egypt, destroying the local religions and massacring those
who resisted them. But in official history writing, this fact is often neglected.
Symptomatic of this cast of mind, Marc Ferro's excellent compilation of texts
on the crimes of colonialism says not a word about the Arab conquest or the
Ottoman Empire. What a hold political correctness can have on us!

Algeria under French control. It's not just that we disapprove, we are now elsewhere. That is why the attempt made
by a certain revanchist Islam, that of the Saudi Wahhabites
or the Muslim Brotherhood, to take over European societies is related to a colonial enterprise that must be opposed.
In Europe, either Islam will become one religion among
others or it will collide with strong resistance on part of
free people for whom the yoke of fanaticism, two centuries
after the French Revolution, is intolerable.

A civilization like that of Europe, which has been guilty
of the worst atrocities and made the most sublime achieve-
ments, thus cannot be seen solely as a curse. If Europe is
motivated by a veritable "genocidal passion,"[5] it has also
made it possible to conceptualize crimes such as genocides,
and after 1945 it distanced itself from its own barbarity in
order to give this word a precise meaning, at the risk of
seeing the accusation turned against it. It is a machine both
for producing evil and for containing it. The peculiar genius of Europe is that it is aware of its dark areas; it knows
only too well what ails it and how fragile are the barriers
that separate it from its own ignominy. This extreme lucid-
ity prevents it from calling for a crusade against Evil on be-
half of the Good and encourages instead a struggle for the
preferable as opposed to the detestable, to use Raymond
Aron's formula. No European leader could say, as President
George Bush did after the attacks on September 11, 2001,
"I'm amazed that there's such misunderstanding of what
our country is about. . . . I just can't believe it because I

[5] Georges Bensoussan, *Europe, une passion génocidaire: essai d'histoire cul-
turelle* (Paris: Mille et une nuits, 2006).

know how good we are." As children of the Old World, we know at least one thing: we are not good (but perfectible). Europe is critical thought in action: since the Renaissance, it has constituted itself within a doubt that denies it and casts on it the eye of an intransigent judge. Western reason is a unique adventure in self-reflection that leaves no idol standing, that gives traditions and authority a pounding. Europe had hardly been born before it rose up against itself and placed the enemy within its heart, subjecting itself to a constant re-examination. If incrimination of the system is to such an extent part of the system itself—if, for example, the whole history of colonialism has from the outset been contested by various schools of anticolonialism—that is because in Europe there is not only a principle of expansion, but also a space of pluralism, of the relativity of beliefs and faiths. To the antagonisms peculiar to nations in a specific geographical area has been added the fundamental element of the internal division within each of them. I do not mean to say that Europe is superior only insofar as it doubts its own superiority. In this respect, however, it differs from other cultures that have not, at least until recently, practiced this systematic challenging of their own convictions. Following the example of the Old World, no people can escape the duty to think against itself.

The Vanities of Self-Hatred

Nothing is more Western than hatred of the West, that passion for cursing and lacerating ourselves. By issuing their anathemas, the high priests of defamation only signal their membership in the universe they reject. The suspicion that hovers over our most brilliant successes always threatens to degenerate into facile defeatism. The critical spirit rises up against itself and consumes its form. But instead of coming out of this process greater and purified, it devours itself in a kind of self-cannibalism and takes a morose pleasure in annihilating itself. Hyper-criticism eventuates in self-hatred, leaving behind it only ruins. A new dogma of demolition is born out of the rejection of dogmas.

Thus we Euro-Americans are supposed to have only one obligation: endlessly atoning for what we have inflicted on other parts of humanity. How can we fail to see that this leads us to live off self-denunciation while taking a strange pride in being the worst? Self-denigration is all too clearly a form of indirect self-glorification. Evil can come only from us; other people are motivated by sympathy, good will, candor. This is the paternalism of the guilty conscience: seeing ourselves as the kings of infamy is still a way of staying on the crest of history. Since Freud we know that masochism is only a reversed sadism, a passion for domination turned against oneself. Europe is still messianic in a minor key, campaigning for its own weakness, exporting humility and wisdom.[6] Its obvious scorn for itself does not conceal

[6] There is even a fanatical form of skepticism that reproduces in its own way the faith that it wants to extinguish: when Cioran writes, for example, that to refuse to acknowledge the interchangeable nature of ideas is to condemn oneself to cause bloodshed, he expresses an idea that is itself not interchangeable with its contrary. Similarly, when the Italian philosopher Gianni Vattimo asks Christianity to understand, in the name of charity, that it is not the sole possessor of truth, that in the intercultural dialogue it must henceforth keep quiet and listen to others, and reconnect "with its univeralist

a very great infatuation. Barbarity is Europe's great pride, which it acknowledges only in itself; it denies that others are barbarous, finding attenuating circumstances for them (which is a way of denying them all responsibility).

Thus it wants to be the sole seat of inhumanity in action and wears this evil disposition as its insignia as others wear their decorations. Even natural catastrophes do not escape our delusions of grandeur: there are always many analysts who see in the slightest hurricane, flood, or earthquake the perfidious hand of Euro-America. Regarding the tsunami in December 2004, some even saw the goddess Gaia rising from the ocean floor to punish our industrial civilization. Like prayer, self-accusation is a way of acting symbolically at a distance when one can do nothing. Megalomania without borders: by attributing all the misfortunes of the world to man, a certain kind of ecology shows an unbridled anthropocentrism that confirms our status as the "master and destroyer" of the planet. To think, for example, that tomorrow we will be able to determine whether we have rain or sunshine, that we will eclipse nature, is to relapse into the Promethean fantasy nourished by the most fanatical adepts of progress. We can, then, contest everything except our own depravity. A blatant case of imperialism in reverse. Decolonization

---

vocation without any colonial, imperialist, or eurocentric implication," he is producing what La Rochefoucauld called an "artifice of pride." This demand for a one-way street is addressed to Islam, Buddhism, or Hinduism; Christianity is thus the only religion that is supposed to recognize the partial nature of its teaching. This amounts once again to considering it the sole religion that agrees to efface itself before others, unique in the way it acknowledges the plurality of beliefs and the relativity of dogmas. Gianni Vattimo, *Dopo la cristianità: per un cristianesimo non religioso* (Milan: Garzanti, 2002).

has deprived us of our power, our economic influence is constantly decreasing, but in a colossal overestimation we continue to see ourselves as the evil center of gravity on which the universe depends.

We need our clichés about the wretchedness of Africa, Asia, and Latin America to confirm the cliché about the predatory, murderous West. Our loud stigmatizations serve only to mask this wound to our self-esteem: we no longer make the laws. Other cultures know it but nonetheless continue to blame us in order to escape our judgment and call us, at the slightest tremor, "people in pith helmets telling other people what to do" (Vladimir Putin). If colonial independence's record of achievement is at present problematic, there is no doubt that someday Africa will take off, and the Arab world as well, that they will cease to be objects of our compassion and become direct competitors, partners on equal terms. Then we will no longer be the "masters of the world" but only formerly well-off people with pale faces. The whole paradox of a sobered-up Europe is that it is no less arrogant than imperial Europe because it continues to project its categories on the rest of the world and childishly boasts that it is the origin of all the ills that beset mankind. Our superiority complex has taken refuge in the perpetual avowal of our sins, a strange way of inflating our puny selves to global dimensions.

It has often been said that decolonization was the detour taken by the countries of the South in adopting the Western world. The planet has modernized itself, no doubt, but it has only partly Westernized itself: it has unified itself

under the triple sign of economics, technology, and com-
munications, not under that of respect for persons or of a
parliamentary system. Even if the number of democracies
is increasing, many governments are still seduced chiefly
by our weapons, our state-of-the-art technologies, and our
large companies that balk at promoting equality or basic
freedoms.[7] To that extent, hatred of the West is still hatred
of human rights and democracy. To welcome the West is to
open the door behind which lurk daring and chaos, challenges to the abuses disguised as traditions and inequalities
based on nature. It imposes on every society insurmountable tasks: freeing themselves from their pasts, emerging
from the reassuring cocoon of custom. It is detested not for
its actual faults but for its attempt to amend them, because
it was one of the first to tear itself away from its own bestiality and invited the rest of the world to follow its example.
It broke the circle of connivance among the violent, and

---

[7] Is Turkey Western? No Muslim state, it is true, has done as much for
secularism, promoted such reforms, engaged in such an upheaval, or shown
such a desire to join Europe. But in moving away from the heritage of Ata-
turk through rampant re-Islamization and by continuing to evade any official recognition of the Armenian genocide, ethnic cleansing of Greeks in
Asia Minor, the crimes of the Ottoman Empire, or the repression of the Kurd
minority, Ankara seems to be practicing a merely superficial democratization out of a simple desire to share in European prosperity. That is what
makes its candidacy for entrance into the European Community problematic, because the arguments for rejecting it balance those for accepting it. In
truth, it is less Turkish ambiguity than European weakness that is troubling;
Europe absorbs countries without enthusiasm and rejects them without passion. Have we forgotten in what a climate of hostile indifference the formerly
communist countries of Eastern Europe were brought into the Union? More
than the equivocations of potential candidates for admission to the Union, it
is our half-heartedness that is the true source of perplexity.

that is what it is not pardoned for doing. As soon as it began to moralize history, it was caught in its own trap, and people began to throw all its wrongs in its face to confound it, especially since it provided the evidence to do so.

In this respect, the true driving force of fundamentalism is less scrupulous respect for tradition than the fear of a way of life based on individual autonomy, perpetual innovation, and the dislocation of authority. Advances in freedom go hand in hand with advances in refusing freedom, especially the emancipation of women, which was a fundamental symbolic change in the last century. Whence the new generations of jihadists born in Europe, those "emirs with blue eyes" in distress in their own society, who are looking for rigid rules that can reassure them. "We are not afraid of death," the suicide bombers say to show their superiority to ordinary people. But they are afraid of life, constantly trampling on it, slandering it, destroying it, and training children still in their cradles for martyrdom. Observers have noted that the photos of terrorists taken a few hours before they made their attacks show people who are serene and at peace. They have eliminated doubt: they *know*. It is the paradox of open societies that they seem to be disordered, unjust, threatened by crime, loneliness, and drugs because they display their indignity before the whole world, never ceasing to admit their defects, whereas other, more oppressive societies seem harmonious because the press and the opposition are muzzled. "Where there are no visible conflicts, there is no freedom," Montesquieu said. Democracies are by nature uneasy, they never realize their ideal; they necessarily disappoint us, creating a gap between the hope they elicit and the realities they construct. They repeat the slanders proffered by their enemies, according them the right to hate them in all sincerity. From the imperfection of our governments, their fundamental perversity is deduced. But we should maintain the reverse: to publicly exhibit our faults is to be conscious of our vices, whereas the real fault is being ignorant of what ails us.

The terrible presumption of the cry "We are civilized!" too often meant, during the imperial period, "We are superior to you." The colonial system could not fail to degenerate into de facto segregation, into an apology for the white race, along with all that presupposes in the way of the mutual debasement of both the native and the colonist. The exportation of violence into distant lands, where it could be practiced without witnesses, allowed the conqueror to abandon laws and rules and turn back the wheel of progress, especially since Europe left this business to its rogues, desperados, and unscrupulous adventurers. But this violence had to be adorned with the culture's forms and alibis to enjoy a total impunity in the name of a superior vocation. Today, being civilized means knowing that one is potentially a barbarian. We Europeans are obviously cowardly and decadent, pathetic in our aspirations and pitiful in our pleasures. At least we are aware enough to try to mend our ways. Woe to the brutes who think they are civilized and close themselves up in the infernal tourniquet of their certitudes.

One-Way Repentance

Here we need to introduce a distinction, classic in philosophy, between repentance and remorse:[8] the former recog-
nizes the sin the better to separate itself from it and to enjoy
the grace of convalescence, while the latter remains in sin
out of a sick need to suffer its burning. Remorse does not
repent of its sin; it feeds on it, wants to remain attached to
it forever. We wallow in "perpetual penitence" (Luther) all
the more insofar as we have not made an act of contrition
and turned over a new leaf. If one cannot change the past,
one can lighten the burden it represents on the memory
of the living. "What has to be broken is the debt, not the
memory," the philosopher Olivier Abel rightly points out.
Whence the importance of public excuses addressed by a
government, an institution, or a moral entity to a nation, a
group, or a minority that was previously persecuted: in this
precise case, words become actions that give rise to concord and point to a possible future. The guilty conscience
is an illness that it would be unfortunate not to have every
time the situation requires it. The worst thing would be to
remain unrepentant in the doubtful circumstances of a
war, a massacre, or a blunder, to be insensitive to the scandalous. Everywhere, the politics of admission, especially if
it bears on a recent event, is preferable to silence; it avoids
prostration and allows us to change our skin rather than
wallow in anguish. People have wrongly made fun of the

---

[8] See, for instance, Vladimir Jankélévitch, "La mauvaise conscience," in
his *Philosophie morale* (Paris: Flammarion, Mille et une pages, 1998), or Jean
Lacroix, *Philosophie de la culpabilité* (Paris: PUF, 1977).

requests for pardon ever since Willy Brandt knelt down in 1977 before the monument to the Warsaw ghetto. A strong government, smart people say, does not lower itself to do such things. On the contrary: it is a proof of grandeur to admit one's errors in order not to repeat them. Words have the power to clarify and to knit the national community together again, on the condition of making amends with temperance, and not lapsing, as now happens, into systematic expiation. Take the example of France: it has long lived under a system of deferred truth, struggling to unveil the secrets that have been fermenting like a puddle of pus for years, because the regalian state, with its twofold Catholic and monarchical heritage, is the depository of the true and the false.[9] The consequence is that it has wallowed in a dark view of its history and for several decades subjected itself to an accelerated catching up in the area of public confession and national castigation. The ankylosis of retention has been followed by a penitential avalanche in which President Jacques Chirac, a great fan of the "first peoples" and a great detractor of Western arrogance, excels. There is always a risk of keeping silent about horrors that have been committed: we perpetuate rancor, arouse monstrous fantasies,

---

[9] It took almost sixty years for France to pay lip service to the Setif massacre in Algeria on May 8, 1945, and longer to officially acknowledge the massacres in Madagascar in 1947. Only in June 1999, thirty-seven years after it ended, did the National Assembly propose the use of the term "Algerian War" instead of "operations for maintaining order in North Africa." As for the responsibility of the Vichy government in deporting French Jews, we had to wait half a century before President Jacques Chirac formulated it publicly. In 1998 Bill Clinton apologized to the authorities in Kigali for the U.S. failure to act during the genocide in 1994. Paris, which was a major actor in this tragedy, has for the time being remained silent.

propagate the reign of suspicion. Marvelous in love, where it encourages all sorts of intrigues, mystery is catastrophic in politics. If in France we strain under the burden of a debt that cannot be repaid, that is because of this indirect relationship to truth, these strategies of evasion that prevent us from explaining ourselves to the world.

The wave of repentance that is washing over Europe and especially our main churches is salutary only if it is mutual, and other beliefs, other systems recognize their aberrations as well. Contrition cannot be reserved for the few and purity attributed, like a kind of moral income, to those who say they have been humiliated. For too many countries in Africa, the Near East, and Latin America, self-criticism is confused with the search for a convenient scapegoat that explains all their misfortunes: it is never their fault; the fault always lies elsewhere (in the West, globalization, capitalism). But this division is not exempt from racism: when tropical or overseas peoples are relieved of all responsibility for their situation, they are at the same time deprived of all freedom and plunged back into the condition of infantilism that obtained under colonialism. Every war, every crime against humanity among the damned of the Earth is supposed to be somewhat our fault and ought to lead us to confess our guilt, to pay endlessly for being a member of the bloc of wealthy nations. This culture of apologies is above all a culture of condescendence. Nothing authorizes us to divide humanity into the guilty and the innocent, for innocence is the lot of children, but also that of idiots and slaves. A people that is never held accountable for its acts has lost all the qualities that make it possible to treat it as an equal. Thus we must enlarge the circle of repentance, open it to all continents, and not confine it to Northern Hemisphere countries alone.[10]

Christianity, Islam: two imperialist religions, persuaded that they know the truth and prepared to save people in spite of themselves, by the sword, by fire, by auto-da-fe. But Christianity, worn out by four centuries of violent opposition in Europe, has had to give ground and admit the principle of secularism, which is, moreover, inscribed in the Gospels. Many crimes can be imputed to the Catholic Church: for instance, having ordered the first genocide in the history of Europe with the massacre of the Albigensians launched in 1209 by Pope Innocent III, in the name of the principle "Kill them all, God will recognize his own";[11] having invented with the Inquisition institutional torture, and state racism with the Catholic queen Isabella's demand for "purity of blood" (*pureza de sangre*);[12] having had all the theological arguments to condemn slavery but having instead justified or at least tolerated it until the beginning of the nineteenth century

[10] The Algerians demand apologies from France before concluding a friendship treaty. Well, let us publicly admit the reality of the dirty war, the use of torture, the brutality of colonization in that country. But let us ask the Algerians to do the same, to unveil their dark side, to clean up their own house. Absolute reciprocity!

[11] Denis de Rougement, *Love in the Western World* (1938), trans. Montgomery Belgion (New York: Doubleday, 1957), p. 109, n. 56.

[12] On the obsession with the taint of Jewish blood in the Spain of the fifteenth and sixteenth centuries and the church's distrust of *conversos*, Jews who had converted to Catholicism, see Bensoussan, *Europe, une passion genocidaire*, pp. 205f.

in order to support the temporal interests of the papacy;[13] having too often spoken in favor of ignorance, madness, and superstition; having killed, eliminated, and persecuted heretics, witches, pagans, and Muslims in the name of love and the true faith. We can also reproach it for the Vatican's indulgent attitude toward the Third Reich when so many German Catholics paid with their lives for their opposition to Hitler's regime. At least Christianity has begun the modernization represented for Catholics by the Vatican II Council (1962–1965). The solemn apologies then made by John Paul II to the Jewish community, the Indians of South America, Orthodox Christians, Protestants, and Africans on the island of Gorée in Senegal, the recognition of the papacy's error in evaluating the main scientific discoveries since Galileo, the condemnation of the Crusades, and the renunciation of forced proselytizing have all marked the culmination of this unprecedented process. And although there remain many dark areas in its history, Rome, like most of the Protestant and Orthodox churches, has begun a courageous critical inventory to bring itself into conformity with the spirit of the New Testament. There are mosques in Rome, but are there Christian churches in Mecca, Jeddah, or Riyadh? Isn't it better to be a Muslim in Düsseldorf or Paris than a Christian in Cairo or Karachi? One would like

---

[13] Not until 1814 did the Catholic Church, in a declaration by Pius VII, officially condemn the slave trade, and this condemnation was given a theoretical justification only in 1888, in a bull issued in by Leo XIII. The enslavement of millions of people in this infamous trade could not be pursued without violating the first principles of Christianity. See Olivier Pétré-Grenouilleau, *Les Traites négrières: essai d'histoire globale* (Paris: Gallimard, 2004), pp. 71–72.

the various European Communist parties, little Leninist groups, Trotskyites, alter-globalists, and ecologists to take a look at themselves and engage in introspection with the same intransigence. But it is always from Christianity and from it alone that repentance is expected,[14] because it invented repentance in its modern forms. In other words, the Catholic Church has simultaneously betrayed and transmitted the spirit of the Gospels. Its long and painful story greatly resembles the moral and political story of the West: the interminable adjustment of reality to principles, which are themselves constantly violated and always reaffirmed. The progress made by reason has been slow but incontestable, even if it has sometimes led to horrible regressions. Decency and dignity have advanced side by side with savagery, the best alongside the worst. Freedom is triumphing, but long after its reign was proclaimed and still only in a few places on the globe. Whatever those disillusioned with progress may think, the collective education of the human race, as it was conceived in the eighteenth century by the German dramatist Lessing, is not an empty expression. It has taken, and will continue to take, the patient labor of history, resistances to be overcome, relapses into tyranny, the awakening of consciousnesses.

---

[14] Witness an astonishing remark by the British journalist Robert Fisk, who questioned whether it was an accident that the pope asked the Jews to pardon him yet didn't feel obliged to ask the same of the Muslims for the bloody and catastrophic invasion of Iraq (*Independent*, quoted in *La Vanguardia*, Barcelona, August 28, 2005). For the record, not only did the Catholic Church not invade Iraq, but it very violently opposed the Second Gulf War, going so far as to receive in Italy the very questionable Tariq Aziz.

This process of questioning remains to be carried out by Islam, which is convinced that it is the last revealed religion and hence the only authentic one, with its book directly dictated by God to his Prophet. It considers itself not the heir of earlier faiths but rather a successor that invalidates them forever. The day when its highest authorities recognize the conquering, aggressive nature of their faith, when they ask to be pardoned for the holy wars waged in the name of the Qur'an and for the infamies committed against infidels, apostates, unbelievers, and women, when they apologize for the terrorist attacks that profane the name of God—that will be a day of progress and will help dissipate the suspicion that many people legitimately harbor regarding this sacrificial monotheism. Criticizing Islam, far from being reactionary, constitutes on the contrary the only progressive attitude at a time when millions of Muslims, reformers or liberals, aspire to practice their religion in peace without being subjected to the dictates of bearded doctrinaires. Banning barbarous customs such as lapidation, repudiation, polygamy, and clitoridectomy, subjecting the Qur'an to hermeneutic reason, doing away with objectionable verses about Jews, Christians, and gays and appeals for the murder of apostates and infidels,[15] daring to resume the Enlightenment movement that arose among Muslim elites at the end of the nineteenth century in the Middle East—that is the immense political, philosophical,

[15] As Eric Conan rightly notes, "The Christian religions were bloodthirsty and murderous by deviating from their texts, whereas Islam was the same by following its text more closely. That is why the partisans of a peaceful Islam propose reforming the Qur'an by purging from it the violent verses against infidels." "N'éteignons pas les Lumières," *L'Express*, April 27, 2006.

and theological construction project that is opening up. Intellectuals, professors, and Arab Muslim clerics have begun to undertake this work (in France, notably Fetih Benslam, Malek Chebel, Latifa Ben Mansour, Mohammed Arkoun, Abdelwahab Meddeb, and Fadela Amara), some of them thereby risking their lives, especially when they are women in revolt against their status (to mention only the most emblematic, the Syrian American Wafa Sultan, the Canadian of Pakistani origin Irshad Manji, the Bangladeshi writer Taslima Nasreen, the German Turk lawyer Seyran Ates, the Dutch politician Ayaan Hirsi Ali). It is time to create a great chain of help for all the rebels in the Islamic world, whether moderate, unbelieving, free-thinkers, atheists, or schismatics, just as we used to support the dissidents of Eastern Europe. But the problem with the moderates is that they are precisely . . . moderate, and never rise to the level of radicals. Europe, if it wants to construct a secular Islam within its frontiers, should encourage these divergent voices, give them its financial, moral, and political support, sponsor them, invite them, and protect them. Today there is no cause that is more sacred and serious or that more affects the concord of future generations. But with a suicidal blindness, our continent kneels down before Allah's madmen and gags or ignores the free-thinkers.

The False Quarrel over Islamophobia

To avoid incurring any blame, in the 1970s fundamentalism invented the term "Islamophobia," which was supposed to parallel xenophobia: this semantic buckler was first used against the American feminist Kate Millet, who was said to be guilty of calling upon Iranian women to take off their chadors, and then in the 1990s against the Anglo-Indian writer Salman Rushdie when he published *The Satanic Verses*.[16] This was a clever invention because it amounts to making Islam a subject that one cannot touch without being accused of racism. Taught for half a century to respect difference, we are asked to avoid evaluating a foreign religion in terms of our Occidental criteria. Cultural relativism commands us to see what we call our values as simple prejudices, the beliefs of a particular tribe called the West. The religion of the Prophet is thus draped in the mantle of the outcast in order to spare it the slightest attack. Islam seems to have forgotten the incredible violence of the anticlerical struggle in France and Europe, which often led to barbarity: churches, temples, and convents burned and razed, priests and bishops hanged or guillotined, nuns raped. The savagery of these reactions reflected that violence carried out by the churches for so many centuries on the people over whom they ruled. It was a battle waged by extreme sectarianism on both sides, but one that freed us from the tutelage of the clergy and forced Rome and the various Protestant denominations to drastically revise their plans to direct the social order

---

[16] On this subject, see two very enlightening books: Caroline Fourest and Fiammetta Venner, *Tirs croisés: la laïcité à l'épreuve des intégrismes juif, chrétien, et musulman* (Paris: Calmann-Lévy, 2003), and Caroline Fourest, *La Tentation obscurantiste* (Paris: Grasset, 2005).

and administer consciences and souls. In France, a country with an anticlerical tradition, one can make fun of Judeo-Christianity, mock the pope or the Dalai Lama, and represent Jesus and the prophets in all sorts of postures, including the most obscene, but one must never laugh at Islam, on pain of being accused of discrimination. Why does one religion and one only escape the climate of raillery and irony that is normal for the others? Let us add that Jewish and Christian fundamentalism are no less grotesque, and that seeing the Republicans in the United States court the most obscurantist and well-organized religious Right is a matter of concern. But apart from the fact that they are not setting off bombs all over the planet, these fundamentalists remain in the minority within their own denominations, where they are restrained by liberals and traditionalists.

To speak of Islamophobia is to maintain the crudest confusion between a religion, a specific system of belief, and the faithful who adhere to it. To attack Islam would thus be to accuse Muslims, and to attack Christianity would be to accuse Christians. But contesting a form of obedience, rejecting ideas one considers false or dangerous, is the very foundation of intellectual life. Must we then speak of anticapitalist, antiliberal, antisocialist, and anti-Marxist racism? Must we refer to some kind of "Christianophobia"? We have a perfect right to do so, to reject all religions, to consider them mendacious, retrograde, mindless. Or must we then re-establish the crime of blasphemy, as the organization of the Islamic Conference demanded during the

winter of 2006, introducing at the United Nations a mo-
tion that would prohibit defaming prophets and imposing strict limits on freedom of expression in the domain
of religious symbols? (Today, because of Islamic censors,
Voltaire's play *Muhammad the Prophet*, a ferocious attack
on hypocrisy and fanaticism written in 1741, can no longer
be staged in France except under police protection.)

The invention of Islamophobia fulfills several functions: to deny the reality of an Islamist offensive in Europe
the better to legitimate it, but especially to silence Muslims
who dare to criticize their faith, denounce fundamentalism, or call for reform of family law, the equality of the
sexes, and the right to apostasy.[17] Thus it is necessary to
stigmatize the young women who want to free themselves from the veil and go out in public without shame,
their heads uncovered; to blast the French, Germans, and
British with family backgrounds in the Maghreb, Turkey,
or Africa who claim first of all the right not to care about
religion, the right not to believe in God, and who do not
automatically feel themselves to be Muslims because they
are of Moroccan, Algerian, Malian, or Pakistani descent.
To block any hope of a change in the land of Islam, these
renegades, these traitors, have to be exposed to the public condemnation of their coreligionists, pointed out, si-

---

[17] An Afghan citizen, M. Abdul Rahman, who converted to Christianity
after a short stay in Germany, was denounced by his family as an apostate
and condemned to death. Under international pressure, the Afghan court
acquitted him on the ground that he was mad (March 27, 2006) and expelled
him from his country.

lenced, told that they are imbued with colonial ideology,[18] and this process has to be anointed by "specialists" duly accredited by the media and public authorities.[19] We are seeing the fabrication on a global scale of a new crime of opinion analogous to the crime that used to be committed by "enemies of the people" in the Soviet Union. It is a question of tracking down a local reformer who wants to "secularize" the judicial system and education, and also of shutting up contradictors, of shifting the question from the intellectual or theological level to the penal level, every objection, mockery, or reticence being subject to prosecution. In short, anti-Muslim racism—attacking a place of worship, for example, which is a matter for the courts—

[18] That is what a French professor, Vincent Geisser, sought to do in *La Nouvelle Islamophobie* (Paris: La Découverte, 2003), which provides a veritable list of the proscribed and traitors to the cause of Islam, journalists, imams, politicians—almost all of them from the Maghreb. There we have a work worthy of a political commissar from the Stalinist period!

[19] Oliver Roy tells us that in public opinion, Islamophobia includes a "rejection of immigration." As for the affair of the caricatures of Muhammad, it has to do with nothing less than "discrimination" on the part of a country, Denmark, where the extreme Right in power "refuses to see Muslims as citizens" [*sic*]. Olivier Roy, *Esprit* (March–April 2006), pp. 323, 327. We know that since the Cold War there has been a syndrome of the specialist who falls in love with the subject he is studying and defends it tooth and nail, even in the worst cases. He cannot allow a single flaw to spoil the splendid object of his passion. The profundity of his knowledge cannot fully conceal certain blind spots in his analysis. We might reflect on the fact that for the past fifteen years the "failure of political Islam" (Olivier Roy, Seuil, 1992) has been announced, at the very time that Islamists have been experiencing immensely increased popularity everywhere, in the Maghreb as well as in Machrek. Driven out by force of arms, they have returned through the ballot box. We know, for example, this sophism cherished in this little milieu: every bomb that explodes is the paradoxical proof of the extinction of the Islamist threat.

is confused with a free examination of doctrine. Just as there is discrimination against people guilty of being what they are—blacks, Arabs, Jews, yellow, white—so the discussion bears on articles of faith, revealed truths, and disputed points that are still open to exegesis and transformation because they themselves are products of a specific history. Islam, especially since the Kemalist revolution in Turkey, is a house divided against itself, wounded by the memory of its lost grandeur, filled with sadness but also with hatred and resentment. The fundamentalists want to close this wound as quickly as possible by attributing it to the Crusaders, to infidels, or to Zionists, whereas the reformers want to open it up further, to recognize it in order to provoke a vital shock.[20]

What is pompously called "Arab Muslim humiliation" is perhaps nothing other than an allergy to diversity, the despairing observation that a large part of the world does not follow the Prophet's teaching, cares nothing for it, and must therefore be punished. We can understand the awkward position of religious Muslims (or Christians) in

---

[20] In Bali, at the summit meeting for a more prosperous Muslim world, which opened on May 13, 2006, the Indonesian president, Susilo Bambang Yudhoyono, after having reminded his audience that Muslims had been the first globalizers, noted with sorrow that among the nations adhering in various degrees to Islam, "there is not one that can be classed as developed according to any criterion whatever. All of them lag behind in terms of knowledge, finances, and technology. . . . The world associates Islam with backwardness. This makes us angry, but the fact remains that we are backward. We are dependent on others for everything connected with our vital needs. . . . Nothing in our religion says that we cannot be developed." On the war within the heart of Islam and the battle for its evolution in Europe, see the very convincing book by Gilles Kepel, *Fitna: guerre au coeur de l'Islam* (Paris: Gallimard, 2004).

an environment that is not religious, their malaise when confronted by billboards that offend their sense of modesty, customs that contradict their prejudices, a freedom of tone, of style, and discussion that is very far from the dogmas of the one and only Book. For those who believe themselves to be the sole depository of Truth, these customs and credos are an insult to God. However, it would be better to internalize Truth and insult God than to massacre people or indoctrinate them by force. We can consider the West's way of life contrary to decency, criticize it, mock it, turn away from it. However, as it exists, in its imperfection, it is not negotiable and seems preferable to what used to be done. We are not going to confine women to the home, cover their heads, lengthen their skirts, or beat up gay people, prohibit alcohol, censure film, theater, and literature, and codify tolerance in order to respect the overly sensitive whims of a few sanctimonious persons. Never was Voltaire's motto *Écrasons l'infâme* (Crush fanaticism and superstition) more to the point. Islam is part of the French and European landscape, and as such it has a right to freedom of religion, proper places of worship, and respect— on the condition that it itself respects republican, secular rules and does not claim an extraterritorial status, special rights, exemption from swimming pools and gymnastics for women, separate education, and various favors and privileges. The best one can hope for it, and in the interest of all, is neither "phobia" nor "philia," but benevolent indifference in a religious market open to all faiths. Happy are the skeptics and unbelievers, if they cool the murderous ardor of religious faith!

They Warned Us!

In 2005–2006 the controversy surrounding caricatures of Muhammad first published in a Danish newspaper resembled a gigantic lapsus. In cities from Jakarta to Beirut, angry crowds paraded through the streets, reminding us of the giant crowds in Nuremberg. They burned down the embassies of Denmark and Norway, attacked French embassies, and killed Christians in Nigeria and Turkey, managing with unconscious malice to see the drawings concerned not as satires in poor taste but as portraits of a redoubtable accuracy. In London, the demonstrators, probably thinking they were showing leniency, carried signs that said "Freedom in Hell," "Get Ready for the Real Holocaust," "Exterminate People Who Mock Islam," and "Europe, Your September 11 Will Come." In Bangkok, an imam interviewed by CNN called for the offending artist to be put to death, or at least to have his sinful hand cut off as a condition for a possible pardon. In Pakistan, a religious leader offered anyone who killed one of the accused artists a million dollars . . . and a car. In Jakarta, demonstrators shouted: "Allah is great, let's hang all the Danes." Were these just expressions of people who had been stirred up by agitators and were acting under the influence of emotion? What all this really meant was revealed by the Iranian president, Mahmoud Ahmadinejad himself: repeated calls for the destruction of Israel, numerous claims that the Shoah was a myth, and finally a threat to wage total war against the West, against "Global Arrogance." Radical Islam constantly speaks two languages: that of the victim, spoken by "respectable" theologians who are sent to Europe and the United States to make us feel guilty, and that of the executioner, who wants to terrorize us and predicts that a terrible vengeance will be taken on us, the annihilation of the impious, of the "Crusaders." We ought to take warning from the adoption of National Socialist rhetoric by extremists in the Near and Middle East. There is no need to accuse Islamo-Fascism of hypocrisy, to find an obscure *Mein Kampf* in some madrasa: everything is said openly. If we don't understand it, that is because we are deaf and blind!

CHAPTER THREE

Innocence Recovered

One mustn't be angry with someone

who has been beaten.

—OSCAR WILDE

Every Way of the Cross eventually leads to redemption. For condemned Europeans, there remains one exit that will allow them to avoid decline: shifting the blame to two nations unworthy of European civilization, Israel and the United States, repudiating them in order to redeem ourselves. Breaking all ties with them, unceasingly renouncing them, calling loudly and clearly, if not for their disappearance, at least for their neutralization, proving that "the West" does not exist, that it is a concept that is not pertinent because it includes dissimilar realities. For those who have lost all their subversive hopes and are not satisfied by the sartorial affectations of Subcommander Marcos, there still remains, to quench their thirst for the absolute, a final noble savage: the Palestinian. He is the great Christ-like icon, the oppressed of the oppressed, whose beatification has been proceeding for the past thirty years. And the fact that his situation has hardly improved makes it possible to keep alive the revolt he incarnates. In 1974 Jean Genet, who praised in his books the beauty of SS men, hoodlums, assassins, Black Panthers, and fedayeen, explained in an interview with Tahar Ben Jalloun: "Why the Palestinians? It was perfectly natural that I should be attracted not only to the most disadvantaged people but also to the one that most fully crystallizes hatred of the West."[1] The point is that the Palestinians, or rather the mythical idea that people have formed of them, conjoin two elements that promote this crystallization: they are poor compared with a handful of colonizers, some of whom came from Europe, and they are

[1] *Le Monde diplomatique*, July 1974.

mostly Muslims, that is, members of a religion that part of the Left thinks is the spearhead of the disinherited. That is how this endless conflict became, between 1980 and 2000, and at a time when revolutionary horizons were shrinking, the incontestable cause of a certain orphaned progressivism. What is surprising about this is that the preference of a minority has become a majority choice, that it has received the assent of the highest spheres of power (at least in France and in Western Europe), to the point that it has shaped the mentality of an era.

How Central Is the Near East?

Nothing is more surprising for an observer than the extraordinary attention the media have given this part of the world for such a long time, as if the fate of the planet were to be determined entirely in a tiny stretch of land between Tel Aviv, Ramallah, and Gaza. The reprobation of Israel is first of all an obsession with Israel. The media's focus is paradoxical, since it tells us, stricto sensu, nothing, limiting itself to reinforcing the stereotype, which is that of a conflict between a colonial, racist state that came into the Arab world at a late date (1948) and a crushed and despoiled people. The treatment of the second Intifada, which began in 2000, was revelatory of this cliché that saw in it a contest between the forces of Oppression and the forces of Resistance. This continuous flood of news items—no day passes without detailed reports on the Israeli army's exactions—has sometimes been accompanied by a massive

misunderstanding of the realities on the ground. On television and in the media we see an *excess of information
that produces ignorance.* How surprising, for instance, to
learn from the Palestinian leaders themselves, the day after
the death of Yasser Arafat on November 11, 2004, that the
militarization of the Intifada had been a great failure and
had left the society exhausted and on the brink of civil war;
that it also led to growing persecution of Christians, who
had been forced to flee or become even more nationalistic,
and revealed Fatah's corruption without decreasing Israel's
morale. A disappointment for the militants, but also for
the press correspondents, who thus found themselves repudiated. What a surprise to learn that old Arafat, who had
had extraordinary luck and had eluded so many traps, had
also proven to be an expert in speaking out of both sides
of his mouth, had embodied the Palestinian national entity
as much as he had sabotaged it by torpedoing the Camp
David negotiations in 2000. Not to mention the demonization of the "butcher" Ariel Sharon (the young Jews attacked in French middle schools during those years were
called *sharognes* [carrion] or *sharognards*), which prevented people from foreseeing the withdrawal from Gaza,
the explosion of Likud, or the declining influence of the
expansionist theses of Greater Israel. The journalists had
not lied, but they had allowed themselves to be blinded by
their convictions: these men in the field had seen in reality
only the projection of their own fantasies.

People who support the Palestinians are not hoping to
aid flesh-and-blood human beings but pure ideas: on the
east coast of the Mediterranean, intellectuals, writers, and

politicians are not so much engaged in inquiring into a specific antagonism—a real estate dispute involving two equally legitimate owners, as Amos Oz put it—as in settling accounts with Western culture. The actual fate of millions of men and women subjected to daily humiliation and pre-carious living conditions is of little importance, as is our indulgence of the terrorism practiced by the Palestinians, Hamas, or Hezbollah. The Near East has become the site of a global battle for the title of pariah. In 1969 Georges Montaron already wrote in *Témoignage chrétien*, an or-gan of the Catholic Left: "Jesus Christ is on the side of the Palestinians, whether they are Muslims, Jews, or Christians, as soon as they are poor . . . they are the refugees, the true holy places in Palestine, the true witnesses to the living God."[2] A few days later, Montaron wrote: "Among all the poor in the Arab world, the Fedayeen are heroes, the living image of the liberator. Like Che Guevara in Latin America, the Palestinian resistance is a flame that lights the way for the oppressed and is gradually spreading. Here, still more than among us, resistance is synonymous with revolution, and it has an incalculable messianic power."[3] Vestiges of a time of enthusiasm, the lyricism of a period we have left

[2] "Jesus-Christ, un réfugié palestinien," *Témoignage chrétien*, December 18, 1969. This Christian view was adopted by some members of Yasser Arafat's entourage. When the headquarters of the Palestinian Authority in Ramal-lah was under siege by Tsahal in 2002, Jibril Radjub, the president's security advisor, declared: "Like Christ's, Arafat's blood will pursue the Jews forever." Another person close to "the old man" said: "The Palestinians are subjected every day to the same sufferings as those endured by Jesus on the Cross." A fine example of rhetorical imitation for the use of a Western public, but one that, in its own way, speaks a truth.

[3] Georges Mantaron and A. Vimeux, *Témoignage chrétien*, December 25, 1969.

behind? Maybe; but in the meantime, many hopes for revenge have been swept away, the conflict has gotten bogged
down, and no other group in the world has supplanted the
infatuation with this one. Consider, for example, what Edgar
Morin wrote on February 19, 2004: "It is true that today the
Palestinians are humiliated and attacked, and that no ideological reason could prevent us from having compassion
for them."[4] The argument is not false, but why should we
forget the Chechens, the Tibetans, the Sudanese in Darfur,
and the Congolese, all of whom have been ignored as if we
were interested only in the victims of a Western country
who have been accorded the honor of a special glory? We
cannot help suspecting that our perception of the Near East
is less political than psychological: it is not a question of doing away with a source of tensions, of reconciling warring
brothers, but rather of pursuing our own mythologies in a
foreign theater.

"Zionism, the Criminal DNA of Humanity"[5]

Two interests converge in this monomaniac obsession with
the Near East: it allows the Arab world to transform the
Jewish state into a convenient diversion from its wretchedness and its frustrations (the rejection of Israel is the
Muslims' most potent aphrodisiac, Hassan II joked), and
it allows part of Europe to clear itself of its past offenses

---

[4] Edgar Morin, *Le Monde*, February 19, 2004.
[5] A slogan adopted by protesters during a demonstration in Paris against
the war in Lebanon, July 30, 2006.

against Judaism. The condemnation of Israel, a veritable leitmotif, especially in the French foreign office, is supposed to be equivalent to an exoneration of the crimes earlier committed against Jews. As if the distant descendants of Jews who were deported to Nazi death camps were now the equivalents of the executioners who gassed their ancestors. *Zionist*: for a long time this adjective was synonymous with infamy in the vocabulary of communist propaganda. Stalin himself used it, along with the term "cosmopolitan," to justify the vast anti-Semitic persecution that was begun in the late 1940s and continued until his death. But the term "Zionist," which has become for the European Left an insult and even an obscenity, has prospered in the Arab Muslim world, which has imported without discrimination all the European anti-Semitic propaganda. What crime has not been imputed to Zionism in the media of these countries? It has been accused of being "a form of racism and racial discrimination," as was affirmed in a resolution adopted by the UN General Assembly on November 10, 1975; it has been accused of having created Hitler out of whole cloth and of having invented the myth of the Holocaust in order to attract juicy business deals. But also of being responsible for the September 11 attacks (Mossad is supposed to have warned all the Jews in New York not to go to work in the towers on those days), of having created the AIDS virus in order to eliminate humanity or the black race, of having caused the tsunami of December 2004 by means of a nuclear explosion, of creating avian flu in order to weaken Africa and Asia, and of having surreptitiously paid for the caricatures of Muhammad published in Denmark in order

to foment conflict between Christians and Muslims, as
Ayatollah Khamenei stated in February 2006. Henceforth,
anyone who considers the notion of a Jewish state acceptable is denounced as a Zionist because Israel is guilty of being such a state. If Zionism didn't exist, it would have to be
invented!

There is no question of minimizing the Palestinian tragedy, denying the illegitimacy of the occupation, or under-
estimating the brutality of the repression, often disproportionate, of the Intifada or the pointlessly cruel destruction
visited on the civilian populations, whether Palestinian or
Lebanese. Nonetheless, it remains that there is something
stupefying about the exclusive focus on this region to the
detriment of others. The state of Israel is far from being
irreproachable; from the outset, it was constructed on the
basis of an expropriation favored by the wars that its neighbors have waged against it, it has had its share of fanatics
and extremists, it maintained perverse ties with the apartheid regimes in Pretoria and Rhodesia, and its army has
occasionally committed terrible blunders, but it is mislead-
ing to treat it as if it were an annex of an evil American
empire.[6] No matter how one approaches it, Israel is always

---

[6] "Because things aren't going well for Israel at the same time that they
are not going well for itself, America approves Israel's increasingly ferocious
behavior toward the Palestinians. . . . The Israelis' increasing inability to perceive the Arabs as human beings in general is obvious to people who follow
the print or television news media. . . . When one abandons the camp of
justice, nothing is more reassuring than to observe others doing evil. What is
unjust about Israel these days does not shock the dominant Western power"
(Emmanuel Todd, *Après l'Empire* [Paris: Gallimard, 2002], pp. 138–39). One
will note the close semantic proximity to the language used by George W.
Bush regarding "evil," even if the term is not applied to the same objects.

supposed to be the troublemaker, the agent of division, the one who impedes universal concord, delays the blessed time of harmony—in short, it is the thorn in the side of humanity. Without it, the world would be better off because this tiny land puts us all in danger. It even constitutes the main threat to world peace, according to a poll conducted for the European Commission in November 2003.[7] We now know that the necessary settlement of the Palestinian problem, that is, the creation in Gaza and the West Bank of a state with recognized borders, will not guarantee peace for Israel any more than it will pacify the crusaders of the Prophet who are waging war against the West. We have to work toward this just end, but without illusions.

What passion is provoked by this confrontation, which is low-intensity compared to African wars whose victims are counted in the millions without much troubling people's consciences! It as if in the world of the media the life of an Israeli or a Palestinian were a thousand, even a hundred thousand, times more valuable than that of an African. Perhaps we should see in this obsession the evolution of our attitude with regard to the Jewish problem in Europe. We have passed from the idealization that followed the revelation of the genocide to the later disparagement. The eulogy carried within itself the imminence of exhaustion; calumny quickly succeeded idolatry. The image of the good Jew, humble and persecuted, was replaced by that of

---

[7] For 59 percent of the people polled, Israel constitutes the chief menace to world peace, and for 53 percent, it is instead the United States. In April 2004 *Le Nouvel Observateur* confirmed this feeling by printing on its cover, under a photo of Bush and Sharon side by side, the headline "The Incendiaries."

the arrogant and aggressive colonist. The former, rootless
and wandering, was admired as exemplary of the human
condition, but the latter, a normal, ordinary citizen of a nation that is fighting for its life, is violently rejected. People
resent the Jews for having emerged from their immemorial weakness and fearlessly resorted to force. They have
thereby betrayed the mission that history had assigned to
them—being a people without a homeland that did not get
tangled up in the obtuse narrowness of the nation-state.
Their dispersion over the world used to be the sign of their
greatness. At a time when Europe itself is repudiating its
fatherlands, the Jews' anchorage in a land that was partly
stolen from others amounts to a disaster. In short, what
people loved in them was not a memory, a culture, a specific relationship to study, to writing, and to the book, but
rather an impersonal, pure, Christ-like projection. What is
their main fault? Without consulting us, the Jews rewrote
the scenario to which we had confined them, and they have
thus lost the right to demand compensation from us. A nation of pariahs, Israel has thus become, in European public
opinion, the pariah of nations. "Israel," said the leader of
the Maurassian Left, "is an advance scout for free-market
colonization." The terms are carefully chosen to combine
two abominations: colonialism and free-market economics. Now all the Jews of Europe are said to be to blame for
the state of Israel unless they have publicly repudiated it.
Through their Manichean coverage of the Arab-Israeli conflict, the media have made the atmosphere unbreathable,
and they bear a crushing responsibility that has produced

the sense of uneasiness they have experienced in recent years. Since the Durban Conference against racism in South Africa in 2000, which led to an orgy of anti-Semitic hatred, the Jew in diaspora has been called upon to proclaim loudly and clearly his aversion to Zionism.[8]

Unmasking the Usurper

According to this view, the true Jew now speaks Arabic and wears a checkered keffiyeh, while the other one is an impostor who claims title to land and has lost "the moral magistracy of martyrdom" (Péguy). The ancient victim has become a torturer in turn, but—and this is the interesting detail—a torturer who reproduces exactly the characteristics of his former tormentor in 1930s Germany. In short, when Jews oppress or colonize, they are immediately transformed into Nazis; there are no half-measures. Israel's affiliation with the invisible Empire of the North and especially with the Yankee Babylon makes it the most faithful reincarnation of the Third Reich. The Nazis persecuted the Jews; then the Jews became Nazis.[9] How else can we explain

---

[8] The philosopher Jean-Claude Milner rightly calls this Jew the "Jew of negation, "the one who, after the gas chambers, says no to Israel and says no to be called a Jew." "The Jew of negation will not shed a tear for a Jewish victim after May 8, 1945." *Les Temps modernes*, November-December 2005–January 2006, pp. 12–21.

[9] As Vladimir Jankélévitch wrote, "Anti-Zionism is in this respect a rare Godsend, because it gives us the permission and even the right and even the duty to be anti-Semitic in the name of democracy! Anti-Zionism is anti-Semitism justified, finally made available to everyone. It is the permission

the spontaneous flourishing of the National Socialist metaphor in the writings of the most brilliant authors? Consider,
for example, the philosopher Gilles Deleuze on the crimes
of Zionism: "People say that it isn't genocide. And yet it is a
history that from the outset has included many crimes like
that committed by the Nazis in Oradour. Zionist terrorism
was not practiced against the British alone, it was practiced
on Arab villages that had to disappear. Irgun was very active in this regard (Deir Yassin)." Regarding the Israeli op-
eration in southern Lebanon in 1978, the same writer says:
"We find ourselves in a situation analogous to that of the
Spanish Civil War, when Spain served as a laboratory and
experiment for a still more terrible future."[10] For those who
are surprised by Israel's imitation of Hitler's regime, it suf-
fices to recall, for example, the close family ties between
the Zionist movement in the 1920s and German National
Socialism, the enthusiastic visit made to Palestine in 1933
by one of the very first Austrian SS men, Leopold Itz von
Mildenstein, and the articles praising Zionism that he
wrote for *Angriff*, Joseph Goebbels's newspaper.[11] In judg-
ing Israel, no distinctions of degree or qualifications are

---

to be democratically anti-Semitic. What if the Jews themselves were Nazis?
That would be great. We would no longer have to feel sorry for them; they
would have deserved what they got." *L'Imprescriptible* (Paris: Seuil, 1986), pp.
19–20.

[10] Gilles Deleuze, *Deux régimes de fous* (Paris: Minuit, 2003). Quoted by
Éric Marty, *Le meilleur des mondes* (Paris: Denoël, 2006), pp. 8, 11.

[11] Plumell-Uribe, *La Férocité blanche*, pp. 277–78. This anecdote is quoted
by Tom Segev, *Le Septième Million: Les Israéliens et le génocide* (Paris: Liana
Levi, 1993), pp. 40–41. This alliance, which was wholly temporary, was
intended to spare the lives of as many German Jews as possible by arranging
their transfer to Palestine.

allowed: in its case, nuances are forbidden, people go immediately to extremes. If Israel withdraws from the Sinai,
southern Lebanon, or Gaza, this is never counted to its
credit. Israel, it is true, has ceased to be the West's moral
creditor; when it took Beirut in 1982, looked on passively
during the massacres in Sabra and Chatila, systematically
colonized the West Bank, severely and even excessively
repressed the second Intifada, targeted extremist leaders
for assassination, built a wall that ate up arable land and
separated families, bombed Lebanon during the summer
of 2006 in response to Hezbollah's attacks, and invaded
Gaza in 2009 to stop Hamas's rocket attacks, it squandered
the international support it initially enjoyed. As the historian Élie Barnavi noted, Israel has lost the battle of the image. But being a democracy, it generally leaves the media
and television free to cover events, including the crimes
committed by its own army. Let us recall that it was in
Tel Aviv that the largest demonstration against Sabra and
Chatila took place and forced General Sharon to resign.
Emmanuel Levinas already said this in 1963: "Israel has not
become worse than the world around it, no matter what
anti-Semites say, but it has ceased to be the best."[12]

Wasted effort: most intellectuals, with the notable exception of Michel Foucault, have devoted themselves to
criminalizing this nation; when they speak of it, the only
the name that comes to mind is Hitler's. Israel is perhaps
the only country in the world about which it is constantly

[12] Emmanuel Levinas, *Difficile liberté* (Paris: Albin Michel, 1963), p. 16.

said that it has a right to exist within secure and recognized borders. This statement is itself stupefying because it immediately suggests the converse: that this right is in itself an exorbitant privilege. The saints of yesterday have been transformed into monsters. In Europe, the Palestinian question has quietly relegitimated hatred of the Jews. Here we can certainly agree with Bernard Lewis when he says that for many of their supporters, "the Arabs are in truth nothing more than a stick for beating the Jews."[13] Further testimony is provided by this extract from an op-ed piece by Edgar Morin, Sami Naïr, and Danièle Sallenave: "The Jews, who were humiliated, despised, and persecuted, humiliate, despise, and persecute the Palestinians. The Jews, who were victims of a ruthless order, impose their ruthless order on the Palestinians. The Jews, who were the victims of inhumanity, show a terrible inhumanity . . . the chosen people is acting like the superior race." "Behaving like a people chosen by God is not only stupid and arrogant, but a crime against humanity. We call that racism," writes the Norwegian philosopher Jostein Gaarder, the author of the famous novel *Sophie's World* (New York: Farrar, Straus and Giroux, 1994), who furthermore suspects some Israelis of premeditating "with the help of God, a final solution to the Palestinian problem" (*Aftenposten*, August 5, 2006). Instant reversibility: if the Jews oppress, they necessarily do so in the manner of the Blond Beast, as faithful reproducers of the abominations they formerly suffered

---

[13] Bernard Lewis, *Le Retour de l'Islam* (Paris: Gallimard, 1985), p. 250.

in Germany and Poland. The simple fact of having been hounded and exterminated by the Nazis transforms them into potential Nazis. The war in Lebanon is assimilated to the German policy of *Lebensraum*, vital space. The Gaza Strip is Auschwitz,[14] and so is Jenin, and Zionism is the twin brother of Nazism.[15] Resistance a posteriori to National Socialism makes it easier to deprive the Jew who does not repent the existence of Israel. This synonymy, with the power to harm that it implies, proceeds from a lamentable theoretical leap made by intellectuals who are supposed to be experts at making distinctions. To Nazify the Israelis is to delegitimize the state of Israel, and it is also to Judaize the Arabs, shifting the ancient battle against ignominy to the banks of the Jordan. Ultimately, it is to justify in advance the possible disappearance of Israel, that "usurping entity."

[14] A cartoon published in Italy in May 2006 by *Liberazione*, the organ of the *Partito della Rifondazione Comunista* (PRC), one of the pillars of Romano Prodi's center-left coalition, shows at the entrance to Gaza barbed wire and a gate over which is the inscription "Hunger will make you free," an obvious allusion to *Arbeit macht frei* over the gate to Auschwitz.

[15] In spring 2002 José Saramago, the Portuguese Nobel Prize winner for literature, visiting Ramallah during the siege by Tsahal, wrote: "In Ramallah I saw humanity oppressed and humiliated as in the Nazi concentration camps." He told a journalist: "What is happening in Palestine is a crime that we can stop. We can compare it to Auschwitz." When the journalist objected, "Where are the gas chambers?" Saramago replied: "They'll be here before long" (*Le Monde*, May 24, 2002). The South American writer Luis Sepúlveda states that "Today as before, we hate the Nazis for what they did to the Jews, Gypsies, homosexuals, and opponents. Now, the Jews will be hated tomorrow for what a warlike cast headed by Sharon did to the Palestinians. In Auschwitz and Mauthausen, in Sabra, Chatila, and Gaza, Zionism and Nazism go hand in hand" (*Une sale histoire* [Paris: Anne-Marie Métailié, 2005], p. 44).

On the Proper Use of Barbarity

Few cultures take so much pleasure as does America in contemplating their defects, in displaying their depravity with a candor that forces us to indulge them. It sometimes makes one think of Freud's remark on "the invading barbarians who killed and then did penance, penance thus becoming a technique permitting murder."[16] The demons buried in the cellars: they are the ones that fascinate us in the United States, that country where everything is visible. The American wager: putting savagery in the service of justice, making evil a necessary ingredient of the good. Since 1945 Europe, on the contrary, has transformed violence into a taboo, a residue of primitive eras, to the point that it has even been suggested that national anthems should no longer be played before soccer matches to avoid arousing murderous chauvinism. However, can one fail to see that soccer and rugby fields are substitutes for the battlefields of old, and that scuffles between fans, or even riots after the game, are preferable to conflicts between infantry and tanks? Europe tolerates violence only by explaining it by social problems, humiliation, or poverty. A repressed barbarity (the Old World) is thus opposed to a restrained barbarity (the New World). But the latter barbarity is poorly restrained if we take into account the aggressiveness of the police forces, persistent segregation, a terrifying prison system, gang wars, firearms, and legalized torture in the army. What is fascinating in America is violence coupled with order (and sentimentality), those highly ambiguous characters, the cowboy, the sheriff, the righter of wrongs, the pioneer, all on the brink of breaking away, plunging into chaos to reorganize the law. So that order itself is never

---

[16] Sigmund Freud, preface to Dostoyevsky's *The Brothers Karamazov*.

simply order, as it is in Europe, but seems always on the point of turning into disorder, of being carried away by uncontrollable violence.

Europe is haunted by the specter of "these explosions of collective bestiality" (Stefan Zweig) that have marked its history for so many centuries. It fears their return. It remembers Diderot's observation that it is easier for an enlightened people to return to barbarity than for a barbarous people to take a single step toward civilization. But to avoid a relapse into inhumanity, perhaps we have to recognize the inhumanity within each of us, rather than deny it? And just as Pascal asked reason to "accommodate its enemy within itself," a democracy must, on pain of languishing away, absorb its contrary without allowing itself to be destroyed by it; colonize to its own benefit values that are hostile to its development, such as rage, intransigence, and fanaticism, and navigate between perils that can kill it but also strengthen it. It has to reckon with violence the better to sublimate it, orient it toward positive ends. America has an amazing ability to live with a dose of structural anarchy, extremism, and chaos that would kill Europeans. So that in America, regularity paradoxically arises from a permanent state of crisis. At the risk of oversimplifying, one might say that two dreams confront each other in our democracies. One wants to eradicate human malice solely by means of dialogue, tolerance, and a constant reminder of past horrors. The other wants to put the bad side of human nature in the service of social perfectibility, and preserve evil's energy in order to divert it toward noble goals. A creative barbarity that seeks to transform hideous passions into generous passions. An angelism of goodness, on the one hand, and containment and sublimation of violence, on the other.

A Delicate Arbitrage

As we know, modern France is torn between two painful memories, that of Vichy and that of the Empire, but they are of unequal weight. Colonization seems a burden less difficult to bear than collaboration, for a simple reason: the defeat in 1940 and the Occupation affected the country as a whole, soiled and debased it, despite resistance by a small and courageous group. Half a century later, our country is still struggling to overcome this trauma.[17] On the other hand, the colonial venture, as brutal and bloody as it often was, and despite having a strong group of supporters in the National Assembly during the Third Republic, ultimately concerned only a small fraction of our compatriots. As is shown by the bitterness of the French colonists who returned from Algeria, the latter quickly came to feel that they had been abandoned by a mother country indifferent to these expeditions. French imperialism, promoted by Jules Ferry, was not based on an overabundance of strength, an excess of vitality, but rather on the fear of decline, a desire to undo the humiliation the country had suffered in 1870, the worry that it was no longer equal to the great European powers. It was a "phenomenon of compensation" (Raoul Girardet) that sought to avoid decline into a mediocre destiny, the whim of an elite obsessed with grandeur and not the desire of

---

[17] See Henry Rousso, *Le Syndrome de Vichy: 1944–1987* (Paris: Seuil, 1987), and Richard J. Golsan, *Vichy's Afterlife* (Lincoln: University of Nebraska Press, 2000).

the national community as a whole.[18] Except in the case of
Algeria, which was a settlement colony, the French pro-
ceeded so half-heartedly in their overseas ventures that the
government had to set up a veritable propaganda office,
the Agence économique des Colonies, whose mission was
to develop "imperial fiber" (*la fibre impériale*) through-
out the country.[19] The shame of the military defeat and of
the Pétain government's participation in deporting Jews
(whereas Denmark, for example, saved almost all its Jews,
and its king is said to have worn a yellow star as a sign
of his solidarity with them) is more keenly felt than the
shame of conquests in Africa and Asia, which most people
now consider the aberrations of another age. Between the
colonial venture and collaboration with Hitler, the latter
is the sin that it is more important to expiate. If it can be
proven that the Jews, once constituted as a state, inflicted
on weaker peoples what they themselves endured at the
hands of stronger ones, then the passivity and even the
complicity of European nations with regard to the Third
Reich is to that extent diminished.

Israel is thus subject to twofold condemnation: as a
Western appendage encysted in the East, it conceals its territorial appetite behind the screen of an insurmountable
wrong, the Nazi genocide, as if the Arabs had to pay for a
crime committed long ago in Europe. The counterpart of
the extreme Right's ancient accusation that the Jews are

[18] Raoul Girardet, *L'Aventure coloniale de la France* (Paris: Pluriel, 1972),
pp. 410–11. See also Marcel Merle on anticolonialism in Ferro, *Le Livre noir
du colonialisme*, pp. 816–61, and the standard work on the subject, Charles-
Robert Ageron, *France coloniale ou parti colonial?* (Paris: PUF, 1978).
[19] Pascal Blanchard, *Le Nouvel Observateur*, November 3–9, 2005.

cosmopolitans is the Left's claim that the state of Israel is illegitimate. So now the hatred of the West finds its vehicle in hatred of the Jews, who have become its emblematic community after having been, for centuries, its scapegoat. Thus the conflict between Israelis and Palestinians is seen as "the symbol of the Western world's denial of the rights of Arabs and Muslims."[20] And thus we also find an incredible tolerance among our intellectual, political, and media elites for Palestinian terrorism: attacks and suicide bombers are condemned, but only faintly, and even justified as acts of desperation, legitimate payback for atrocities committed by the Jewish armed forces. In their view, no horror committed by candidates for suicide, with their grotesque mythology of the seventy virgins awaiting them in Paradise, will ever make up for the ignominy of the Israelis. The victims of these explosions matter little, and still less the culture of death spread among the youth of the West Bank and Gaza. Our indulgence is deeply imbued with condescendence: we don't ask whether the encouragements sent out by militants hiding in their European or American bastions isn't suicidal for the Palestinians themselves or burdens their desire for peace and decency, because there are "moments when peoples aspire to raise their children somewhere besides a cemetery" (Jean Daniel).[21] Our fascination, through the mediation of television screens, with the bloodbaths, collective executions, and redemptive martyrdom of Hamas of Islamic Jihad is not merely pornographic, as was

---

[20] Pascal Boniface, *Le Nouvel Observateur*, May 12, 2005.

[21] In Germaine Tillion, *Les Ennemis complémentaires* (Paris: Éditions Tirésias, 2005), preface by Jean Daniel.

Baudrillard's jubilation at the collapse of the twin towers in New York. Above all, it proves our scorn for this people that has been reduced to being simple human projectiles. We obviously prefer the aesthetics of crime to the ethics of compromise.[22]

And, finally, that is how the French intelligentsia and part of the Left, despite a vigilant antifascism that has been raised to the level of a Republican mystique, have kept silent when confronted by the wave of Judeo-phobia of immigrant origin that has washed over France since the beginning of the second Intifada (and in the context of which occurred the torture-murder of the young Ilan Halimi by a gang from the suburban housing projects in 2006, mixing violent crime with racism). Many of them got mired in an embarrassing denial, when they didn't accuse the persons involved of paranoia or even provocation.[23] It is symptomatic that every time France is at odds with its own identity

[22] On the excitement and almost titillation the human bombs provoke in the intelligentsia, see Paul Berman's excellent analysis in *Terror and Liberalism* (New York: Norton, 2003), chap. 6, especially on the examples of Breyten Breytenbach and José Saramago.

[23] The book by the philosopher Alain Badiou, *Circonstances 3, Portées du mot "Juif"* (Paris: Éditions Lignes, 2005), bears witness to this mentality. In it, the author compares the state of Israel, as an archaic state, to Pétain's France and describes it as "the external form, of a colonial nature, taken by the sacralization of the term 'Jew,'" a state that is supposed, moreover, to be planning the genocide of the Palestinians. For Badiou, who adopts here the Catholic Church's traditional anti-Judaism, the true Jew is the one who has to cease to be a Jew and merge with other people. For him, to say that one is a Jew is immediately to trigger an anti-Semitic passion. This leads inevitably to a twofold conclusion: Israel has to be eliminated and the Jews asked to erase themselves as such, to become goys like everybody else. The true Jew is one who aspires to his own disappearance. On Badiou's book, see especially Éric Marty and Alain Badiou, "L'Avenir d'une négation," *Les Temps modernes*, winter 2005–2006.

it attacks its Jews, even if these days it does so through the prism of the Near East. This is an emotional relationship: France almost revolted to defend the reputation of Alfred Dreyfus, who had been accused of treason. "A country capable of splitting itself in two over the honor of a little Jewish captain is a country where we have to go as soon as possible," the father of the future philosopher Emmanuel Levinas told him on the eve of the Second World War.[24] But even since 2000, the guardians of the dogma of resistance, who track down everywhere the slightest trace of indulgence toward Nazi doctrine, have been transformed into accomplices of the vexations, insults, and blows inflicted on their Jewish fellow citizens. Nothing comparable, of course, with the 1930s, just enough trouble and suspicion to poison everyday life. There has been no lack of authorized spokesmen to explain the events by the context, such as the amiable José Bové, who, on Karl Zero's television program, accused Mossad of burning down synagogues in order to foment turmoil (he later apologized for having said things that might "wound people's sensibilities"). When the political scientist Pascal Boniface, in a note to the leaders of the Socialist Party in April 2001, advised them, as a matter of simple electoral calculation, to abandon the Jewish vote (500,000 in France) for the Muslim vote (five million), he very honestly spilled the beans.[25] Forced to takes sides

[24] Quoted by Alexis Lacroix, *Le Socialisme des imbéciles: Quand l'antisémitisme redevient de gauche* (Paris: La Table Ronde, 2005), p. 38.

[25] In this note, Boniface, the director of the Institut de relations internationales et stratégiques (IRIS), warned the leaders of the Socialist Party and the government of Lionel Jospin to abandon their pro-Israel sympathies, which threatened to alienate the Muslim vote. Shortly before, during a visit

between two minorities, many intellectuals who are active sympathizers with the Palestinian cause have preferred, in the name of a strict antiracism, to abandon the Jews for the Arabs, considering the former as unjustly favored and the latter as unjustly disinherited, and thus writing off the Jews' feeling of loneliness and abandonment. The acts of violence, and the fact that in France, many men and women can no longer walk the streets of a city wearing a kippa or a Star of David, that Jewish children can no longer go to any school they please, have been excused by referring to the malaise of the young in the projects. The latter have been left free to take out their frustrations, in small doses, on those weaker than themselves.[26] No, Europe has not returned to the violent outbursts of the period between the two world wars; it has even erected all sorts of moral and legal barriers to prevent a return of the foul beast. But on occasion it is capable of practicing an anti-Semitism by abstention in the name of a praiseworthy concern for equity and tranquility. (That does not, however, prevent it from showing an equivalent racism with regard to immigrants from North Africa or Black Africa or committing ignoble attacks on foreigners of color.) How can we forget, in this context, the anecdote about the British officer in Palestine in 1947 who, witnessing the daily

---

to the Near East, Jospin had described Hezbollah as a terrorist movement. In political science, the "Boniface theorem" has become a term describing clientelist practices. This appears as an appendix to Boniface's book *Est-il permis de critiquer Israël?* (Paris: Robert Laffont, 2003). A strange title that one might turn around: Is it permitted not to criticize Israel?

[26] "Hitler would have made a good Muslim," a student said to his teacher who, shortly after September 11, was telling his class in a school in northeast Paris that Hitler had killed six million Jews. "An Entrenched French Problem: Antisemitism," *International Herald Tribune*, March 24, 2006.

confrontations between Jews and Arabs, was unable to decide which of the two groups he despised most? Someday, in order to avoid importing the Israeli-Palestinian conflict into their communities, the mayors and government leaders of all the great cities of the Old World will have to decide between large Muslim communities and small Jewish ones. We dare not imagine which one they will abandon. When faced by vociferous minorities supported by a strong external diaspora, social tranquility is worth a few sacrifices.

America Doubly Damned

For its detractors, the empire of evil is bicephalous: it functions in tandem, through the mutual cultivation of the same defects, in Washington and in Jerusalem. While Europe relieves itself of the crime of the Shoah by blaming Israel, it relieves itself of the sin of colonialism by blaming the United States. Evil America condenses in a single place, a single people, and a single system all the abjection of which Europe used to be capable. Parasitical, murderous, arrogant, America seems to bear all the signs by which we recognize the West's guilt: as rich as it is inegalitarian; dominating, polluting, and founded on a double crime, the Indian genocide and the Black slave trade; prospering only by threatening military intervention; liberal in words but protectionist in deeds; indifferent to the international institutions to which it pays lip service, it is entirely devoted to the worship of the almighty dollar,

the only religion in this materialist country. And for years
the America of George W. Bush offered the hallucinating
spectacle of a great Western power embarking again, in
the name of the war on terrorism, upon the imperialist
enterprise in Iraq and Afghanistan, at a time when all
European governments have abandoned it. In order for
the Old World, stained with its age-old sins, to be able to
recover its lost virginity at the expense of its transatlantic
big brother, the American Satan has to play several contradictory roles: it has to be close enough to us to combine
the traits we detest in ourselves, but far enough away not
to conceal an unbridgeable gap. Thus it has to be the black
sheep of the family, the dishonoring progeny, the canker
lurking in the heart of the West. Like anti-Semitism, an
allergy to "minimal alterity" (Vladimir Jankélévitch), the
hatred is addressed to a close associate whose intolerable
proximity is disavowed. America is a double of Europe,
perhaps, but in the sense in which the healthiest parents
can give birth to abnormal children and dream about
committing infanticide. From that point on, our malaise
ceases to tend toward self-flagellation and is projected
onto this providential third party, the symbol of absolute crime. Like a cruel mother repenting her sin, Europe
wants to recover its virginity by symbolically killing its
transatlantic child, the latter concentrating in itself all the
negative characteristics of its countries of origin. (That is
why in Europe anti-Americanism is a veritable passport
to notoriety: it won the 2005 Nobel Prize for literature for
the British playwright Harold Pinter, a ferocious detractor

of Bill Clinton and George W. Bush who was also a member of the support committee for Slobodan Milošević, and in 2003 it won for Michael Moore the Palme d'or at the Cannes film festival for his documentary *Fahrenheit 911*.)

And for a declining Europe that is no longer an actor in history but only a spectator, what a comfort to see the most powerful army in the world frustrated by a handful of jihadists in Iraq; what a fine revenge to take on the New World, which was deaf to our warnings and intoxicated by its certainties. The phobia of America, our last civic religion in Western Europe, allows us to escape our guilty conscience by affiliating ourselves with formerly colonized continents. France, Germany, Spain, and Italy, having become political dwarfs, seem to proclaim in the public eye: we are divorcing ourselves from the West in order to come closer to the South, with which our interests are identical. "Allow an intellectual, even if he seems to be on the Right, to quietly say why he feels himself in strict solidarity with the Third World . . . , why he thinks European culture and the Western way of life are now distinct entities, why he hopes and wants to believe that the struggle of the future will be summed up in the formula: Europe and the Third World vs. the West."[27]

The expression "the West" has had a strange fate, rejected by the extreme Right and the extreme Left, and vituperated by the Nazis even if a few small groups were able to use it. In European nationalist propaganda, it has always signified the evil that comes from the west:

[27] Alain de Benoist, *Europe, Tiers-Monde, même combat* (Paris: Laffont, 1986).

from Dostoyevsky, a militant Slavophile who contrasted Holy Russia with the "accursed liberal dregs," to Thomas Mann defending, in his 1914–1918 *Diary*, the German soul against the mechanical civilization propagated by France and America, not to forget Heidegger, who distinguished the dehumanized world of technology, incarnated by the USA and the USSR, from German authenticity.[28] So that each European country can be the West for the others, and Europe as a whole can project this concept onto America alone. On the left, "Western Civilization" means the failure of modernity, the devastation of the globe, the erasure of the specific features of minorities, the enslavement and massacre of peoples. Beyond this common pathos, there is in the idea of the West a twofold nature, philosophical and geographical. Focusing only on the latter, we can, like Samuel Huntington, ask the West to renounce all intervention, to stay home and to avoid the clash of cultures. Conversely, if we privilege the first aspect, the notion contains an explosive charge, a semantic wealth that overthrows the order of things, extends far beyond our continents, and merges with the emancipation of the Enlightenment.[29]

[28] "The planet is in flames. The essence of man has become unhinged. World-historical thought can come only from Germans, on the condition that they find and defend their 'Germanness.'" Lecture on Heraclitus delivered in the summer of 1943, *Oeuvres complètes*, vol. 55, p. 123. Quoted and translated by Luc Ferry.

[29] Thus for Jürgen Habermas the opening up of the German Federal Republic is the "greatest intellectual achievement of our postwar period," the only one that authorizes constitutional patriotism while keeping Germany from lapsing into Central European ideology. *Devant l'Histoire. Les Documents de la controverse sur la singularité de l'extermination des Juifs par le régime nazi* (Paris: Cerf, 1988), p. 57.

Decoupling the Old and the New Worlds is also the strategy pursued by Al-Qaeda and the Iranian president, Ahmadinejad, who promises the Old World indulgence if it behaves well and renounces the New World. How many European countries would be prepared to obey that injunction, since they derive their main claim to glory from their resistance to Uncle Sam? Excommunicating the American cousin is a way of showing that after centuries of errors, we have finally gone over to the good camp of the oppressed and the resisters. Being one of the vanquished, writing history from below, that seems to be our dream. We may realize it sooner than we think.

Bounty Bars, Oreos, and Uncle Toms

Converting stigmata into a privilege: that was always the reflex of the dominated, the defeated, the slave. "I call upon my face the splendid glory of spittle," Aimé Césaire said magnificently. Proletarians, vagabonds, pariahs, gays have all taken pride in being condemned and praised the beauty of the degraded, the vilified, the maligned, of those who see in their decline the promise of a redemption. But in being proud of what one is, isn't there a risk of once again transforming skin color into a barrier separating Good from Evil? Melanin vs. vitiligo: all the perjurers, all the traitors will then be called Bounty Bars, Oreos, Uncle Toms—black on the outside, white on the inside. Disagreements are once again racialized: if a black person thinks differently from others, he thinks like a European, that is, he is necessarily "white," a valet who is a ventrilo-quist, a traitor to his brothers. Then he will be treated like "a scab in an ethnic labor union" (Jim Sleeper)[30] devoted to defending the sectarian interests of a specific commu-nity. How then should we categorize mixed-race people, mulattos, quadroons, octoroons, swarthy people, all those who feel neither black nor white and whose indetermina-tion throws fanatical classifiers into a panic? If one wants to knock down the old prejudice that associated, among Muslims and Christians, black skin with a black soul, the "Curse of Ham" is capital.[31] But must we for all that make negritude or Africanness a mode of thought and action, see a fundamental connection between an individual's

---

[30] Jim Sleeper, *Liberal Racism* (New York: Viking, 1997). Quoted in Faes and Smith, *Noir et français*, p. 385.
[31] A religious justification that explains the enslavement of the blacks by a biblical text: Genesis 9:20–27.

genetic background and his intellectual or moral qualities, or otherwise redistribute the attributes of inferiority
and superiority? Is there a black reason, a white reason, a
war of epidermises? Since when does biology determine a
person, unless we go back to twentieth-century postulates
of colonial thought and "scientific" racism? Progressive
thought is blind when it suggests that there can be no an-
tiwhite racism or an anti-Semitism among the formerly
oppressed or the young people in the projects because
they themselves have suffered from this evil. They are the
victims; they are exempt from the prejudices that affect
the majority of the population. But the reverse is true:
racism is multiplying at exponential rates among groups
and communities, taboos are collapsing, and everything
is explained in terms of physical characteristics, identity,
purity, and difference. And this is a racism that is all the
more certain that it is right because it is regarded as a legitimate reaction on the part of the persecuted. Now we
see the obsession with the pedigree and the old distinctions derived from slavery being revived, and prejudices
accumulating in the name of racism. This is the end of
the concept of humanity as union in diversity and the triumph of human species incompatible with each other.

CHAPTER FOUR

The Fanaticism of Modesty

Old men like to teach good precepts

in order to console themselves for

no longer being able to give bad examples.

—LA ROCHEFOUCAULD

A Tardy Conversion to Virtue

We too often forget that contemporary Europe was not born, like the United States, from a collective commitment to regard everything as possible. Europe was born out of its weariness with sacrifice. It took the total disaster of the twentieth century for the Old World to be won over to virtue, like whores whose age leads them directly from debauchery to religious zeal. Without the two world wars and their train of horrors, its desire for peace, which coincides with a desire for repose, would never have come into being. It was our saturation with murder and criminal immoderation that led us to abandon savagery for good behavior. We may behave better, but it is the good behavior of animals that have had their fill, are tired of butchery, and are resigned to less far-reaching projects. (In this respect we might hazard the following hypothesis: so long as the repression of instincts was the rule in the West, the most aggressive nations compensated for this repression by means of colonial or military expeditions. Once this censure was lifted, the spirit of peace prevailed, and desire could henceforth be realized on the personal level, satisfying itself without enslaving.) European democracy makes us think of the convalescence that peoples who used to be excessively turbulent impose on themselves after they have lost the taste for battle: democracy by little steps, "constructive modesty" (Pierre Rosanvallon) in contrast to the imperial political religion[1] that democracy has become in

[1] Consider these words of Pierre Rosanvallon (*Le Monde*, February 22, 2005): "The dogmatic universalism that goes hand in hand with the

the United States. In Europe, democracy is what remains when all other dreams have been abandoned: a very diverse space in which one can live well, realize oneself, and perhaps get rich in proximity to cultural masterpieces. An admirable ambition, to be sure, since this kind of government limits the damage to human lives, abstains from violence, and is wary of all forms of proselytizing in matters of human rights. This calm would be perfect in a time of great serenity, in a world in which "perpetual peace" (Kant) finally prevailed. But there is a striking contrast between the idyll that Europeans tell each other they enjoy—the rule of law, dialogue, respect, tolerance, multilateralism—and the tragedy that the world all around them is experiencing: Russia is autocratic, Iran aggressive, the Near East in tatters, Africa unstable, North Korea threatening. Europe no longer believes in evil, it knows that disputes can be settled by concertation. It no longer loves history: the latter is a nightmare, a minefield from which it first emerged, with great effort, in 1945, and then again in 1989 after the fall of the Berlin Wall. It wards off this poison by means of norms, rules, procedures. And since

conception of democracy as a political religion contains an unbearable arrogance that is only increased by its spontaneous naïveté. In contrast, democracy conceived as an experiment opens the door to a true universalism, an experimental universalism. By recognizing that we are all apprentices when it comes to democracy, this approach allows us to inaugurate a much more egalitarian dialogue among nations! Democracy is an objective to be realized—we are still far from constituting a society of equals and a collective control over things—not a capital we already possess. Europe has often been very distant from such a constructive modesty. But only if it makes itself the champion of such a philosophy will it be able to make its voice heard and help America become aware of the deepest reasons why it is out of tune with the world."

history continues on its way without us, the Old World leaves to others the task of taking charge of it, while violently criticizing these others for their archaism. The old commitments are finished; every time a dispute arises, we procrastinate, temper our indignation with cynicism, and reject both the aggressor and the aggressed. We show the clairvoyance of the coward who swears he won't give in to provocation. When America mobilizes and acts (often with a tragic lack of awareness), Europe stands by with its arms folded. A timorous colossus at risk of developing gigantism, losing in effectiveness what it gains in extension, Europe is in danger of becoming the Pontius Pilate of nations.

The Empire of Emptiness

Sartre once said that he couldn't get along with the Americans because they didn't believe in original sin. However, North America also experiences, especially on the Left, this guilty conscience with regard to the Indian genocide, slavery, and persistent segregation. It had much to overcome, since Lyndon Johnson's Civil Rights Act, which put an official end to racial discrimination, dates only from July 2, 1964, almost a century after the abolition of slavery and the end of the Civil War. It has taken forceful steps in the schools, in business, and in public transportation to attenuate the consequences of these terrible tragedies, to the point of becoming the country that sets the standards for minority rights. If the United

States remains haunted by the dark pages in its short history, it has moved with extraordinary swiftness, especially since the Vietnam War, to atone for them. Its humiliating defeat at the hands of the Viet Cong inflicted on the imperial republic a trauma from which it has still not fully recovered. Since that time, investigative reporting that is prompt to detect abuses, torture, and massacres has helped it denounce crimes almost as soon as they are committed, looking its bad side squarely in the eye, in the best Protestant fashion. But if it sometimes sinks into self-deprecation, America retains its ability to combine self-criticism with self-assertion. As the victor, along with its allies, over Nazism and then communism, and as the leader of the fight against Islamism, it can be proud of its recent history, despite its flaws. In America, perhaps because each new generation effaces the preceding one, passivity never erases the dimension of the future, while Europe spontaneously covers itself with ashes and wallows in orgies of masochism. American citizens proclaim a pride in their country that we often lack on this side of the Atlantic.

Tocqueville already observed that Americans have "a very high opinion of themselves" and are "not far from believing that they form a separate species within the human genus." There is in America a fusion of patriotism with the sacred, whereas Europe remains a desperately secular construction. When America has doubts, these seldom extend to the ideals of its Constitution, which are on the contrary invoked as inviolable precepts to condemn those who govern badly. The American dream is thus reborn from the worst errors and survives all reports of its death. Europe, on the other hand, has no worse enemy than itself, its hectoring guilt complex, scruples pushed to the point of paralysis. How do we expect to be respected if we no longer respect ourselves, if we never cease to describe ourselves, in the media and literature, in the most negative terms? The truth is that Western Europeans do not like themselves enough to overcome their disgust and show with regard to their culture the fervor that is so striking in the United States. *America is a project, Europe is a sorrow.*

Consider our common currency. What do bills of 10, 20, 50 or 100 euros represent? Arches, bridges, doors, as if our continent were no more than a transit point, a waiting room, a hand held out to the rest of the planet. The figures of Shakespeare, Cervantes, Rembrandt, Leonardo, Goethe, Dante, Pascal, Voltaire are gone. All these men are DWEMs, Dead White European Males, to use the terminology in vogue on certain campuses, and they are suspect, still tainted by prejudices that our triumphant modernity has swept away. Europe or the triumph of "substantial vacuity" (Ulrich Beck), the height of disincarnation. Its past is cursed: it has to repudiate it at all costs in order to become only a movement toward others, a pure idea that can transcend national borders. Besides, in this domain extreme modesty goes hand in hand with gluttony because some people are already dreaming, with territorial excess, of bringing Azerbaijan or Brazil into the European Union. The old imperial fantasy is not dead. But it has become a formal gigantism constructed on an abstraction that declines any historical or geographical depth, any affective memory.

The Pacification of the Past

In 2005 a Royal Air Force pilot who had bombed Dresden in February 1945 (35,000 dead) participated along with others in making donations to reconstruct the bells and crosses of the city's cathedral, the Frauenkirche, which had been entirely destroyed. The reconstitution was to be identical to the original: nothing took place, the war was just a bad dream, the sons repaired the errors of the fathers. The past has the double characteristic of being both over and incomplete. It is constantly changing, constituting perhaps the only dimension of time over which we have any influence: "no one knows what yesterday will consist in," people joked during the Stalinist period, when every year the authorities rewrote history to suit their needs. Now we want to freeze it, subject it to a kind of ethnic cleansing. Like a murderer trying to erase the evidence of his crime, Europe is involved in a great retrospective cleansing. It is polishing, cauterizing, shaping, embalming: for example, the face-lifted Auschwitz in Roberto Benigni's film *Life Is Beautiful*, or the sterilized Paris in *Amélie Poulain*. Perhaps we will soon see committees of virtuous citizens petitioning to change the names of our streets, erasing the names of the fiendish kings, princes, ministers, and military men who have blood on their hands—and they all do! The overwhelming accumulation of memories and sorrows in a single space gives rise to the fantasy of a great cleanup: for instance, "slamming the door on the sick twentieth century," as the Hungarian prime minister, Orban, said in 2002. In that way we will give ourselves a posteriori a history we won't have to blush for.

The positive aspect of this mentality is that it has preserved Europe's heritage with a praiseworthy degree of excellence. We protect our villages, our historical sites with maniacal attention to detail, a concern to make them fit into the landscape, which is itself carefully groomed and arranged and constitutes all the beauty of the Old World. Even a city like Paris, which is so sublime, romantic, and still imbued with literary substance, and which used to represent an extreme concentration of strengths, is in danger of being turned into a museum and resembling a copy of the nineteenth century more than a world capital. This is the grammar of nostalgia: we suspect that in our forward progress, something essential has been left behind, and that it is important that we preserve a few traces of it. We try to give our public squares and private mansions the patina of the immemorial. Like old men who collect newspapers, letters, and knickknacks, we archive, pile up, and constantly extend the list of monuments to be preserved—belfries, cathedrals, castles, or low-cost housing buildings.

However, this nostalgia seeks less to revive the flickering flame of memory than to extinguish it forever. It transforms us into tourists in our own history, and in palaces and ancient cities we take pleasure in contemplating a specific quality of the time: pacification. These

convents and fortresses that bear witness to distant fren-
zies and raging passions confirm our belief that barbarity
belongs to past eras, that history will never come back.
Restoration amounts to a second burial that is analogous,
mutatis mutandis, to decommissioning a nuclear reactor
by pouring tons of concrete on it. Far from maintaining a
living, complex relationship to the past, far from making
a leap into "the liberating abyss of tradition" (Heidegger),
we take from it the weapons we need to protect ourselves
against its possible return. We like it when we can cajole
it, when the conflicts have ceased and the wounds have
healed over. Then comes a pause whose main quality is
that it has ceased to importune us. Our hearts ache when
we contemplate an abandoned church, whereas two hundred years earlier, we would have burned it down or pil-
laged it, perhaps out of hatred for the clergy. These battles
are over; ecclesiastical property has become part of the
cultural domain. The past is a great leveler: we grant amnesty to the victors and to the vanquished, to the tormentors and to their victims; we have moved beyond all those
quarrels. We take pleasure in the melancholy of these ruins, a promise of calm and immobility. One site is as good
as another, they are all picturesque and ravishing; we can
prefer one period or another, at our leisure, it makes no
difference. Every fervent European sooner or later falls in
love with Rome, Venice, Prague, Vienna, Athens, Krakow,
or Granada, manifesting Stendhal's syndrome: a sensation
of choking on the excess of masterpieces. The hypertro-
phy of the world of yesterday, the great Greco-Roman,
Arab-Andalusian, or Austro-Hungarian mausoleums,

all these ancient stones, in their splendor, overwhelm us, suffocate the future, and petrify us in turn. There, lives have already been lived, fates sealed, engraved on marble. These Baroque or Romanesque splendors don't say to us: Dare! Instead, they command us: Respect, repeat. Europe as a sarcophagus: it wraps itself up, like Christo's objects, in the great drapery of preservation. But it does so the better to conjure its demons: to commemorate is to exorcise. Making a tacit oath: never again history and its mass destructions, never again anything but private life, the twists and turns of consumerism, the obsession with happiness. A strange inversion: the past, which is naturally fragile and doomed to sink into darkness, takes precedence over the present and the future, transforming the living into visitors to cemeteries. That is the great difference between Europe and America: one broods on the past, the other starts over again. America, like a snake shedding its skin, starts over on new bases every ten years. It lives in the permanent inauguration of itself, devoting itself entirely to the cult of possibility, to the religion of the future. Europe, on the other hand, inoculates its children with its guilty conscience and conceives its survival only as an escape from the torments of humanity.

The Guilty Imagination

The true crime of old Europe is not only what it did in the past, but what it is not doing today—its inaction in the course of the 1990s in the Balkans, its scandalous wait-

and-see attitude in Rwanda, its silence on Chechnya, its indifference to Darfur and western Sudan, and in general its indulgence, its kowtowing, its servility.[2] What is remarkable in this regard is the way Europe avoids getting involved in current tensions, including those on its own soil, leaving it to the Yankee big brother to do the dirty work, while criticizing him harshly later on. Whatever America does, whether it intervenes or stands aside, it is always wrong, in accord with the customary roles. In the Near East or elsewhere, Europe, like Hegel's "beautiful soul" who does not want to soil the splendor of his interiority, refuses to dirty his hands except to hold them out with passionate effusiveness to all men of good will. When the latter reject our friendship, we leave it to others to do what has to be done. We have seen this in Bosnia in 1995, in Kosovo in 1999, and in a caricatured form in 2002, when the European Union requested the mediation of Washington and Colin Powell to settle the microscopic dispute between Spain and Morocco over the tiny island of Perejil near Tangiers. It was noted with alarm in the winter of 2006, during the affair of the caricatures of Muhammad, when the European Union, booed by the crowds in Damascus, Gaza, Jakarta, Teheran, and Beirut, shamefully failed to support Denmark and Norway, condemned the blasphematory drawings, and sent Javier

---

[2] Cf. Jacques Chirac: "Arab leaders sometimes use methods that differ from ours. But I refuse to judge political systems by the yardstick of our traditions in the name of some sort of ethnocentrism. Moreover, I must say that a multiparty system does not seem to me necessarily desirable in developing countries." Quoted in F.-O. Giesbert, *Jacques Chirac* (Paris: Seuil, 1987), p. 486.

Solanas to the Near East as a traveling salesman for expiation. If tomorrow Vladimir Putin set his big paw on the Baltic countries, invaded Georgia, or set up a puppet regime in Moldavia, Western Europe would cry in unison: "Take what you want!" Only the United States, possibly, would react. We can deplore this fact; but everywhere a people is oppressed and groans in its fetters, everywhere it endures the burden of tyranny, it still turns toward America for relief, not toward Europe. Even the Palestinians, despite their hostility to Washington's policies, know that they have a better chance of someday having their own state with Washington than with Paris, Berlin, or Madrid.

On the whole, the Old World prefers guilt to responsibility: the former is easier to bear; we get on well with our guilty conscience. Our lazy despair does not incite us to fight injustice but rather to coexist with it. Despite our intransigent superego, we delight in our tranquil impotence, we take up permanent residence in a peaceful hell. This verbal despondency is an act that allows us not to feel obliged to justify ourselves to anyone. Remorse is a mixture of good will and bad faith: a sincere desire to close up old wounds and a secret desire to retreat to the sidelines. There comes a time when moral and metaphysical culpability is used to elude any real political responsibility. The debt to the dead wins out over the duty to the living. *Repentance creates people who apologize for ancient crimes in order to exonerate themselves for present crimes.* A cautious withdrawal to the fortresses of the North, a renunciation of the duty to spread the democratic idea and to contain barbarity. Culpability closes Europe to everything that differs from it, makes it an actor in an intimate tragedy from which it cannot escape. "Leave us alone!" said some banners held by protestors against the war in Iraq in 2003. What an admission: they want to cut all ties with the world if these ties are going to be a source of tension! It is in reality the fear of contagion that animates these pacifists, and not concern for the Iraqi people.

Nothing is more insidious than the idea of a collective sin that is supposed to be handed down from generation to generation and to permanently stain a people or a community. Contrition is not a policy. There is no more a hereditary transmission of the status of victim than there is a transmission of the status of tormentor: unless we create a crime of filiation, the "duty to remember" does not imply the automatic purity or corruption of the great-grandchildren. History is not divided into sinful nations and angelic continents or cursed races and inviolable peoples, but rather into democracies that recognize their despicable acts and dictatorships that conceal them by draping themselves in the faded garments of martyrdom. It hardly needs to be said that Africans, like Asians or the French, are solely responsible for their development and can blame only themselves if they lag behind, no matter how harsh the international system may be (even if in certain cases the pillaging of wealth by foreign companies occurs with the complicity of local authorities, and even if one has to militate for debt cancellation). Through their struggle, formerly colonized peoples have become actors in their destiny; they are therefore accountable for their acts and cannot forever blame their problems on the former colonial powers or attribute their errors to a "colonialism without colonists" (Marc Ferro), a notion that irresistibly evokes the famous knife without a blade that lacks a handle (Lichtenberg). There are no innocent states: that is what we have learned in the course of the past half-century. There is no state that is not founded on crime and coercion, including those that have just appeared on the stage of history. But there are states capable of recognizing their barbarity and seeing it for what it is, but who are instead seeking in their former oppression excuses for their present malfeasance.

Recovering Self-Esteem

One part of the world, ours, is thus obsessively preoccupied with drawing up a list of its crimes and creating a lofty statue of itself as a torturer. From childhood on, we are taught to reprimand ourselves. The critical passion whose function was to free the individual from prejudices has become a widely shared prejudice. But beyond a certain threshold of vigilance, reason is transformed into a destructive skepticism. When doubt becomes our only faith, it begins to denigrate all the energy that faith used to put into veneration. Then we refuse to defend our societies: we would rather abolish ourselves than show even a tiny bit of attachment to them. This is a double error: by erecting lack of love for oneself into a leading principle, we lie to ourselves about ourselves and close ourselves to

others. It is a mistake to think that self-devaluation is going to open us up, as if by a miracle, to distant peoples,
put us on the track of goodness and dialogue. In Western
self-hatred, the Other has no place. It is a narcissistic relationship in which the African, the Indian, and the Arab
are brought in as extras in an endless drama about settling
scores: and that is why we are witnessing the conjunction
of remorse with racism, of affliction with the stalest egoism. The automatic nature of the self-flagellation barely
conceals our insensitivity or scorn for faraway cultures
(which we like only if they remain traditional and authentic, that is, archaic). The bitter raillery is extended to the
rest of humanity and makes it impossible for us to love another person. How could we admire the grandiose metaphysics of Sufism, Hinduism, or Buddhism, how could we
understand foreign traditions if we begin by trampling on
our own in a sort of militant ignorance that looks a lot like
vandalism? Let us beware of anyone who values the foreigner only out of disdain for himself: his self-aversion will
end up infecting his sympathies. Let us become friends of
ourselves so that we can be friends again with others. We
make a mediocre use of the world when we are weary of
our own existence. Thus Europe contemplates with sorrow the pile of garbage that it has become for itself, "that
valley of dry bones" (Hegel) that is its history. But it reads
this history in a partial and deliberately taciturn way because it sees only one aspect of it: the worst. This memory
that torments it is in fact very selective and resembles amnesia. It simply forgets that it consists of more than "rivers
of blood and mire"; there is also the progress of the rule of

law and democracy. Since the Romantic period, we have had a melancholy view of civilizations: we muse about the fall of the Roman, Byzantine, Ottoman, and Austro-Hungarian empires, and for us, every historical formation is destined one day to return to dust and ruin. We forget the inverse phenomenon: the resurrection of peoples and nations. The attempt has been made to make Germany and thus Auschwitz a metaphor of contemporary Europe, bearing the mark of Cain, bent under the weight of an insurmountable turpitude. But nothing indicates that Germany is doomed to eternal shame when it has regained its place in the concert of nations and recovered an easygoing patriotism after an exemplary effort to reflect on itself (today, Germany's Jewish community is the third largest in Europe, after those of France and Great Britain). In 1945 an impartial observer would have described it in terms of an accursed country, unrecoverable, doomed to decline. In his novel *Doctor Faustus*, which he had begun in 1943, the novelist Thomas Mann, who was then living in exile in the United States, wrote:

> Now the torture-chamber has been broken open, open lies our shame before the eyes of the world. Foreign commissions inspect those incredible photographs everywhere displayed, and tell their countrymen that what they have seen surpasses in horribleness anything the human imagination can conceive. I say our shame. For is it mere hypochondria to say to oneself that everything German, even

the German mind and spirit, German thought, the
German Word, is involved in this scandalous ex-
posure and made subject to the same distrust? . . .
How will it be to belong to a land whose history witnesses this hideous default; a land self-maddened,
psychologically burnt-out, which quite understand-
ably despairs of governing itself and thinks it for
the best that it become a colony of foreign powers;
· a nation that will have to live shut in like the ghetto
Jews, because a frightfully swollen hatred round all
its borders will not permit it to emerge; a nation that
cannot show its face outside? Is the sense of guilt
quite morbid which makes one ask oneself the question how Germany, whatever her future manifesta-
tions, can ever presume to open her mouth in human affairs?[3]

Roosevelt was convinced that the Third Reich was con-
spiring "unrestrained against modern civilization's rules
of decency,"[4] and the Morgenthau plan envisaged the total dismemberment of Germany so that the latter, once it
had capitulated, would be forever weakened, dislocated.
Everything changed with the arrival of Harry Truman in
April 1945 and the beginning of the Cold War: having become a rampart against communism, Germany ceased to

[3] Thomas Mann, *Doctor Faustus*, trans. H. T. Lowe-Porter (New York: Knopf, 1948).
[4] Quoted by Aleida Assmann, "De la culpabilité collective," *Le Débat*, no. 124 (March–April 2003), p. 175.

be demonized, and its rights were gradually restored. Who had ultimately triumphed over whom? Didn't the military defeat on May 8, 1945, turn out to be a gift to the Federal Republic of Germany, a deliverance and the beginning of a new departure, an opportunity to carry out on itself a true labor of introspection, the proof that a people is never bound inseparably to its abominations and can exorcise them, rejoin the human family?

Let us recall this very simple fact: Europe has more or less vanquished its monsters, slavery has been abolished, colonialism has been abandoned, fascism defeated, communism brought to its knees. What continent can boast of such a record of accomplishment? In the end, the preferable won out over the abominable. Europe is the Shoah plus the destruction of Nazism, it is the Gulag plus the fall of the Wall, the empire plus decolonization, slavery and its abolition—each time, a specific form of violence has been not only transcended but delegitimized. This is a double progress of civilization and law. We are not talking here of falling into extreme nationalistic pride (Yoshinori Kobayashi[5]) of the kind defended by the extreme Right, which seeks, by a series of approximations, to provide a glorifying vision of history: this school asserts the grandeur of a country despite its crimes, but we have to be proud of ourselves *against* our crimes because we have recognized them and rejected them. Freud described melancholy as a problem with self-esteem: to a suspension of interest in the world

[5] Quoted by Régine Robin, *La mémoire saturée* (Paris: Stock, 2003), pp. 170–71.

and a loss of the ability to love is added an increasing tendency to self-reproach that can go so far as "the mad expec-
tation of punishment." In our case, this mad self-belittling
forgets that in the end freedom won out over oppression,
and that is why we live better in Europe than people do in
many other places. A nation cannot forever identify with
its torturers, its traitors, and its hoodlums, or sanctify its
citizens who were defeated, shot, or martyred. It must first
of all celebrate its heroes and heroines who, at the most
critical moments, dared to resist and allowed a people to
recover and move forward with their heads held high. It is
their example of which we have to show ourselves worthy.
Let us think of Herodotus's injunction: history began to be
written in Greece so that people's lofty deeds might not sink
into oblivion. These exceptional beings were themselves
ambiguous, embarked upon dubious enterprises. There is a
strong temptation to criticize them retrospectively, the better to desanctify them: democratic individualism, with its
passion for equality, is averse to greatness, seeing in it a fatal
residue of aristocracy. It is forever reducing extraordinary
people to the level of the average person. It likes to repeat
Hegel's famous statement that "no hero is a hero to his valet." But it forgets the rest of the quotation: "not, however,
because the hero is not a hero, but because the valet is—the
valet."[6] This leveling urge extends even into the past, where,
like psychological valets, we doggedly examine great figures
in order to cut them down to size. Only victims receive our

[6] G.W.F. Hegel, *The Phenomenology of Mind*, trans. J. B. Baillie (1910; rpt.
New York: Harper Torchbooks, 1967), p. 673.

compassion; our pantheon is composed only of the afflicted or defeated, and we compete with each other in weeping over them.

The Twofold Lesson

History offers us a twofold lesson: that a people can die, and that a people can be reborn, that human communities sometimes emerge from the worst aberrations greater than ever before, providing us with examples of admirable resurrection. Two philosophies thus conflict in us: one is a source of fear and despair, the other a source of courage and endurance. The former overwhelms us with the irremediable, the latter frees us from it and calls upon us to reject fatalism. Confidence is like taking chances and prophesying, it is a will to take responsibility for our own future, an aptitude for leaping beyond doubt and fear, for gathering strengths we didn't know we had. In Spinoza's terms, it is an increase in power, the certainty that the world is a secure place where I can develop myself fully. To recover confidence is to rediscover capacities for action that multiply by themselves, whereas excessive cautiousness gives rise to fear and a shriveling of ambitions. The only debt we owe to people we have persecuted, apart from the recognition of these persecutions, is to promote the extension of democratic regimes or at least to accelerate the erosion of despotism. Our obligation is not to remain silent, out of embarrassment, when these same peoples fall in their

turn into arbitrary rule or oppression, but to prevent everywhere the return of humiliations and butchery. Let us recall
Raymond Aron's observation, which the whole work of the
great Indian economist Amartya Sen seems to illustrate: the
main obstacle to development is not the economic system,
no matter how harsh it might be, but rather the lack of freedom, of a sense of the public interest and concern for public
welfare. Europe has to have done with fanaticism and modesty: if it cannot swallow up the world with a big spoon,
it has to take its share and remain the singular voice that
speaks for justice and law, and acquires the military and
political means to make that voice heard. This responsibility increases in the degree that we also assume that democracy draws sustenance from the belief in democracy when
it bears and incarnates its values with determination. If it
limits itself to moderation alone, it is in danger of exhaust-
ing itself. Penitence is ultimately a political choice: that of
an abdication that in no way immunizes us against wrong.
The fear of returning to our former errors makes us too indulgent with regard to contemporary infamies. The crime
of interfering is replaced by the crime of indifference.

   In a famous passage in his *De rerum natura* (at the beginning of Book 2), Lucretius imagines the wise man sit-
ting on a cliff watching men who have imprudently gone
to sea and are perishing in a storm. "It is sweet to see what
misfortunes one has escaped." But what if the cliff falls into
the sea? By preferring injustice to disorder, the Old World
risks being swept away by chaos in its turn, the victim of a
wisdom that is another name for renunciation.

What Is the Penitence-State?

When the state is transformed into the grand master of rites of expiation—kings used to have the privilege of pardoning, whereas modern presidents have the privilege of making apologies—when the cold monster becomes compassionate, usurping the spiritual role of moral authorities and the scientific competence of academic authorities, it seeks to carry out a reconciliation, to exhume a troubled past in order to prevent its return. It often succeeds all too well, to the point of falsifying the meaning. Universal repentance is contemporary with the final age of a state, that of its collapse: then it pretends to get involved in everything, writes history instead of letting historians write it, claims to be the guarantor of inviolable truths. Righting wrongs retrospectively, it busies itself with settling old accounts in order to inscribe them in the list of the national conscience's responsibilities. This prolix repentance substitutes for real action and ends up in a confusion of orders and legislative panic. A frantic concern with memory is not a symptom of totalitarianism, but rather of a muddled effervescence, a refusal to lead.

Since 1968 we have moved from a republican state that practiced top-down reforms to a liberal state that has to respond to the aspirations of civil society (Luc Ferry). It is this latter state, impatient to transform things, that is now imposing change. Here we see the state reduced to the role of an arbitrator between diverse interests. This should make us happy because the democratic ideal is based on the dream of a strong people and a weak government. But then we realize that the people is also weak and divided. The state becomes society's self-consciousness in all its contradictions. In the state, society sees not a serene image of its unity but rather a mirror of its rifts. The more it castigates itself, the more it excites the greed of pressure groups only too happy to emphasize their grievances and to try to establish fiefs and baronies for themselves, if necessary with parliamentary support. In the nineteenth century, Tocqueville had already observed that the government had taken the place of Providence. Must it also take the place of conscience? Make itself a spokesperson for opinions? Then a mad mortification grips the highest spheres: henceforth they order only a single calendar, that of mourning; every month, every week must bleed at the memory of our crimes. Has not a day commemorating the massacre of the rebels of the Vendée in 1973 recently been required? Why stop there? There is no social, professional, or regional category that could not plead some wrong, some distant massacre that must immediately be included in the list of commemorations. We think we are engaging in a therapeutic ritual, preventing rancor and vengeance; in fact, it is the other way around—we are awakening the rage of those who have not been mentioned, and eliciting an epidemic of claims: How about me? and me? But the state is not a church, it has to deal with the present and the future, not spend its time atoning. When President De Klerk, handing over power to Nelson Mandela in July 1994, made a solemn apology for apartheid, he was supporting a process that was under way and putting an end, through his words, to a specific repression. He was acting as a politician and not as a penitent, and he did not disassociate regrets from action. There is a danger involved in overdoing requests for pardon, especially when they concern events that occurred centuries ago. Such requests musts remain exceptional and be surrounded by a certain majesty, on pain of becoming reduced to "the oblique genuflection of a pious person in a hurry" (Flaubert).

CHAPTER FIVE

The Second Golgotha

A history which is designed only for Jews (or
African Americans, or Greeks, or women, or
proletariat, or homosexuals) cannot be a good
history, though it may be comforting to those
who practice it.

—ERIC HOBSBAWM

History, or rather the history that we Germans
have repeatedly mucked up, is a clogged toilet.
We flush and flush, but the shit keeps rising.

—GÜNTER GRASS

We have to admit it: more than sixty years after the Third Reich's capitulation, the pedagogy of the Shoah has failed. After so many books, films, and debates, we have ended up with a situation at the beginning of the twenty-first century in which the genocide of the Jews and Gypsies can no longer be taught in many French schools! What happened? A saturation effect, a feeling that the Jews were monopolizing all the suffering in the world? Probably, and the multiplicity of commemorations has helped make the Jews seem a problematic elect that arouses jealousy. A fine example of an expression of sympathy that is turned against its beneficiaries, turning them into mimetic rivals who have to be driven out in order to take their place. We know that the omnipresence of discussion of the Shoah in France since the 1980s is explained by the long silence that followed the return of the surviving Jews in 1945, when the traumatized nation wanted to recognize only members of the Resistance or those who were deported because they had fought against the enemy. The racial crime was minimized; only the *maquisards* had a right to have a red carpet rolled out for them. The equation has been reversed. Auschwitz, smothered under its own success, has become the West's true "civil religion," our primal scene; as the Hungarian writer Imre Kertész put it, kitsch took it over and killed it. The event was detached from its context and rose over the century like a dazzling star. The survivors became icons of a quasi-metaphysical experience that elicited all kinds of strange glosses. This is a redoubtable sacralization because there is a danger that the Jews will be once again sacrificed on the altar of this cult of which they are the transitory idols. The proof of this is that extreme Islamists treat the Shoah as a belief, a "confusion of fact with faith" (André Glucksmann), the conflation of a historical event with a precise liturgy. If some people dare to criticize Moses, Jesus, Vishnu, Muhammad, or Buddha, why then should we not laugh at Dachau, Bergen-Belsen, and Treblinka? A sinister amalgam: it would never occur to anyone to make fun of the St. Bartholomew's Day massacre, Louis XIV's persecutions of the Protestants, the Palestinians killed during the Intifada, or the Armenian and Rwandan genocides.

Misinterpretations of Auschwitz

It is not too much to say that Auschwitz drives people crazy, producing both law and madness. It has become the gold standard for human suffering, the "new Golgotha" (John Paul II), as if Christ had died a second time there. Retrospective posterity: history has been reread on the basis of Auschwitz, it has taken the past permanently under advisement, created new penal qualifications. The suffering of the Jews has become the universal measure of suffering, and its particularities—pogroms, diaspora, genocide—are claimed by everyone. But it has also given rise to a calamitous misinterpretation: it fascinates people not as an abomination but as a treasury from which it is thought advantages can be drawn. We have not so much sensitized public opinion to a major abjection as we have fed a perverse metaphysics of the victim.[1] Auschwitz has become a monstrous object of covetous lust. Whence the frenzied effort to gain admission to this very closed club and the desire to dislodge those who are already in it. Whence also the convergence of all suffering in Auschwitz, which becomes the desirable horror par excellence, the one whose heir everyone wants to be in order to experience an unparalleled destiny: occupying this most prized position becomes, for some people, an obsession, as is shown by the imposters or deranged persons who pass themselves off as survivors of the Nazi camps.[2]

The victim madness has done so much damage that for some people the concentration camp uniform has become a garment of light. A trivialization of genocide? It is exactly the reverse. Everyone is fascinated by this absolute evil and lives in its redoubtable shadow: in this sense, a revisionist is not someone who does not believe in the Shoah; a revisionist does not even believe in Jews (or, in other cases, in Cambodians, Armenians, Bosnians, or Tutsis) and would like to replace them with more "deserving" groups: Palestinians, Hutus, Serbs, etc. It is an introversion of the dead, not of the event. What people want to strip from the victim in order to clothe themselves in

[1] I refer here to my analysis of this phenomenon in *La Tentation de l'innocence* (Paris: Grasset, 1995), part 2, on competition in victimhood. See also Shmuel Trigano's incisive essay *Les Frontières d'Auschwitz: les ravages du devoir de mémoire* (Paris: Livre de Poche, 2005).

[2] Like the Swiss Binjamin Wilkomirski, a genius of falsification, who pushed fraud very far, or the Spaniard Enric Marco, who told his story in schools and on television for years before he was unmasked by a historian in 2005.

it is the moral eminence, the tragic splendor it seems to enjoy. Suffering gives one rights, it is even the sole source of rights, that is what we have learned over the past century. In Christianity, it used to generate redemption; now it generates reparations, which imply three elements: a broadening of the range of the intolerable (offenses that used to be accepted are now condemned), an end to impunity for criminals, and finally, the sacredness of the victim. In our age of loudly displayed enjoyment, affliction still runs the show. Anyone who seizes control of it also seizes power. The great superiority of unhappiness over happiness is that it provides a destiny. It alone distinguishes us, enthrones us in a new aristocracy of the outcast. An unprecedented mental register: one has to display one's own distress and if possible eclipse that of one's neighbors in order to be recognized as the most meritorious.

In this respect, we can see the Shoah in two ways: as a negative theology that makes Jews the agents of an accursed election or as a concept providing access to the understanding of mass crimes. There were genocides long before 1942, and the whole history of humanity is in a sense the history of a crime against humanity. Since Nuremberg, the exterminations of the American Indians, the Australian aborigines, and the Armenians have been seen differently, and it was Hitler's abominations that made colonial oppression intolerable. This process was not solely a manifestation of the justice of the victors, it was creatively productive, as Karl Jaspers saw as early as 1946: it marked the beginning of a new penal order. Never had an event led to so broad an interpretation, to the point of being claimed by forces hostile to one another. It is one thing to say that Jewish suffering blazed the trail and made it possible to conceive our own, and another to say that it conceals our misery and must be evicted. We know that in France as in the United States, within the Democratic Party, blacks and Jews have long shared in a common solidarity of the excluded. Frantz Fanon, a writer and psychiatrist from the Antilles, liked to repeat the words of his philosophy professor: "When you hear people speak ill of the Jews, prick up your ears—they're talking about you." An anti-Semite necessarily hated blacks. This unity, in proportion to the divergent destinies of each community, has been shattered on both sides of the Atlantic: the Jew is no longer a "brother in suffering" (Frantz Fanon) but someone whose tragedy tarnishes mine and prevents me from being his brother. It is as if other peoples, competing with Jews for the privilege of annihilation, were to shout: "Auschwitz is us!" The fundamentalist preacher Tariq Ramadan, an advisor to Tony Blair, has said that Muslims today are comparable to the Jews of the 1930s. That is, to criticize Islam is to put on the uniform of a Nazi killer.[3] Wounded memories compete for the title of most

---

[3] In England, Sir Iqbal Sacranie, the secretary-general of the Muslim Council of Britain, has proposed the replacement of Holocaust Memorial Day by Genocide Day: "The message of the Holocaust was 'never again' and for that message to have practical effect on the world community it has to be inclusive. We can never have double standards in terms of human life. Muslims feel hurt and excluded that their lives are not equally valuable to those lives lost in the Holocaust time." Among the victims of the "Arab Muslim genocide" he includes the Palestinians and the Iraqis, but not the Kurds gassed by Saddam Hussein.

affronted. Today, who does not fight to claim this capitalized label, "Genocide," whose semantic radioactivity is intact? What government, what country does not seek to seize this qualification in order to take its place on the grandstand where only the most privileged sit?

Hitlerizing History

You may not know it, but Hitler preceded himself by several centuries in the history of humanity. The Third Reich is not the regime that came to power in the elections of 1933 and disappeared in the ruins of Berlin under the hammer blows of the Red Army and the Western Allies in May 1945, it is in a sense the matrix of European history or, to put it another way, its true face. Thus more and more historians claim for blacks, for Arabs, and Native Americans the jurisprudence of anteriority. "There is a dynamic relationship between the destruction of the natives of America, the annihilation of the Blacks, and the policies of extermination introduced by the Nazis in Europe during the first half of the twentieth century," writes Rosa Plumelle-Uribe.[4] In 1955 Aimé Césaire was already warning the

> very distinguished, very humanistic, very Christian bourgeois of the twentieth century that he bears within himself a Hitler of whom he is unaware, that

[4] *La Férocité blanche*, p. 23.

Hitler inhabits him, that Hitler is his demon, that if he scorns him, that is because he is illogical and because ultimately what he cannot forgive Hitler is not the crime in itself, the crime against man, it is not the humiliation of man as such, it is the crime against the white man, it is the humiliation of the white man, and having applied to Europe colonialist procedures that had previously been applied only to the Arabs in Algeria, the coolies in India, and the blacks in Africa.[5]

That is also what we are told by Claude Ribbe, a member of the national advisory commission on human rights, when he compares Napoleon to the Führer; Napoleon was guilty not only of having reestablished slavery but also of having prepared "the industrial extermination of a people" and instituted "racial legislation that prefigures the Nuremberg laws":

A hundred years before the Shoah, a dictator, hoping to make himself the master of the world, did not hesitate to crush part of humanity under his boot. I am not speaking of Hitler, but of his model, Bonaparte. How have the exactions of this misogynist, homophobic, racist, fascist, anti-Republican despot, who detested the continental French as much as he detested the Corsicans, been able to remain unknown to the general public up to now? Why has a certain part of France stubbornly sought,

[5] Aimé Césaire, *Discours sur le colonialisme* (Paris: Présence africaine, 1955; rpt. 2004), pp. 13–14.

in the twenty-first century, to make the butcher of the "Blacks" a national hero?[6]

Another historian, Olivier Le Cour Grandmaison, who tells us in a book with the significant title *Coloniser, exterminer*[7] that the methods used to pacify Algeria—massacres of prisoners and civilians, roundups, destruction of crops and villages—served as a laboratory for creating new concepts, those of a "race without value" and "vital space," which were destined to be used later on in the way we all know. He exhumes the 1846 writings of a certain Eugène Bodichon, a physician and a passionate advocate of the extermination of inferior races—starting with Arabs—in the name of progress, and explains that it was in fact there, in the sweet humidity of the colonies, that was imagined, long before the destruction of the Jews of Europe, a coherent project of genocide, to adopt the neologism forged in 1944 by the Polish lawyer Raphaël Lemkin.[8] A paradigm shift: the colonized peoples of Cochin-China, West Africa, and Algeria subjected to exorbitant rules by the legal code

[6] Claude Ribbe, *Le Crime de Napoléon* (Paris: Editions Privé, 2005), quoted in Richard Senghor, "Le surgissement d'une question noire en France," *Esprit* (January 2006), p. 15. What is surprising about this approach is the retrospective illusion, the semantic anachronism, the description of a man of the early nineteenth century in the vocabulary of contemporary evil: death squads, triage camps, etc. How can Bonaparte be a fascist when the word and the phenomenon did not exist? On this episode, see Yves Benot, *La Démence coloniale sous Napoléon* (Paris: La Découverte, 1992), and Thierry Lentz, "Bonaparte, les Antilles et l'esclavage colonial," *Commentaire*, no. 13 (spring 2006), pp. 127ff.

[7] Olivier Le Cour Grandmaison, *Coloniser, exterminer: sur la guerre et l'État colonial* (Paris: Fayard, 2005).

[8] Ibid., p. 123.

for the natives prefigure the status of Jews under Pétain.[9] In short, total war is not to be sought in the "storms of steel" (Ernst Jünger) that ravaged Europe between 1914 and 1918, nor in the Führer's plan, launched on June 21, 1941, to annihilate the Soviet Union; it has its direct source in the mountains of Kabylia in the nineteenth century, which were in the hands of French soldiers who killed, ravaged, annihilated, and decapitated with a regularity that makes a chill run down your back.[10] The penal system under which the "natives" of Algeria lived, subjected to exorbitant fines and to the system of collective responsibility, was in fact that of totalitarian terror in Nazi Germany:

> Whether in the Reich or in Ancienne Régence in Algiers, racial groups, considered as embodying a constant threat to public order in the case of "the Arabs," and as "natural enemies" of the government in the case of the Jews, were condemned, independently of their opinions and behavior. As for the punishment meted out to them, it was motivated not by what they had done but solely by what they were supposed to be: guilty by birth.[11]

Olivier Le Cour Grandmaison, under cover of impartial scholarly work, is set upon a single objective: by means of a retrospective prophecy, to attach the little caboose of the conquest of Algeria to the great train of the Shoah, to transpose term for term its vocabulary, its atmosphere,

[9] Ibid., p. 339.
[10] Ibid., p. 338.
[11] Ibid., p. 217.

its spirit. To prove that in both cases there was premedi-
tated savagery. To show, for example, that when Bugeaud
or Saint-Arnaud smoked out the rebel tribes, they were
not committing unpremeditated acts but administra-
tive massacres, the forerunners of the techniques of
cold-blooded liquidation later used in the Second World
War.[12] Everything that began in the colonies, in the form
of extreme brutality, is supposed to have flowed back to
the home country to set up iron regimes. And when the
author describes the repression of the riots in June 1848
in Paris, which soldiers who had come from Algeria led
with the same ferocity they displayed in North Africa, and
makes an analogy between colonial wars and social wars,
he yields to the temptation to transform the class struggle
and the labor movement into a genocidal adventure: the
lower social strata are conceived as races or quasi-races to
be eliminated in their turn.[13] Marx better watch out: the
exploitation of man by man was in fact only an extermination of man by man. The birth of capitalism, the uprooting
of millions of starving people from the countryside, their
mass entrance into the hell of factories and manufactur-
ing, children working in the mines from the age of five,
high mortality, unhealthiness, alcoholism, poverty: it is
easy to imagine what a historian who is in a hurry and
has a taste for sensationalism might write, painting a vast
fresco of the history of the labor movement as a prefigu-
ration of National Socialism, the bosses playing the role
of Gauleiters, the foremen that of the kapos. It will come

[12] Ibid., p. 141.
[13] Ibid., p. 282.

to that! Olivier Le Cour Grandmaison yields here to the
sin of retrospective intention: it is one thing to discover
in European colonialism the antecedents of twentieth-
century totalitarian regimes—as did Hannah Arendt—
and another to postulate an equivalence between these
different phenomena, to read the past as a detailed, logical,
and ineluctable preparation for the disasters that occurred
under Hitler and Stalin.[14] To do so is to forget that these
two regimes did not consist in a simple recapitulation of
old dictatorships but made a break with everything that
history had known up to that point. They constituted, in
the strict sense of the term, an entirely original invention.

Europe was its own tormentor before it went outside
itself and forced America, Asia, and Africa to serve its desires. Have we forgotten that war on our own continent,
even if it was conceived and codified in a legal way, was
rarely a matter of courtliness, a chivalric exercise; that
most battles involved havoc and carnage, mass killings,
ruined cities, starving peoples put to the sword, women
and children included, and everywhere ruin, terror, deso-
lation, and exquisitely cruel tortures? Have we forgotten
the macabre bloodletting of torture under the Old Regime,
the dramatization of corporal punishment, the fate of

---

[14] A psychiatrist, also mentioning Hannah Arendt, has already used the
Nazi metaphor to describe the factory and the office as quasi-detention
camps, places of "evil" where the managers are the collaborators, and the
employees the Jews! (Christophe Dejours, *Souffrances en France: la banalisa-
tion de l'injustice sociale* [Paris: Seuil, 1998]). In 1968 students styled themselves "intellectual workers." Now they see themselves as in a precarious
situation, that is, as pariahs: the transition from the status of worker to that
of victim simple signals the end of workers' culture and the triumph of the
deported victim in the social imagination. This is a major conceptual shift.

men thrown in prison or sent to the galleys? Is it reasonable to treat the conquest of Algeria as a "disquieting precedent" for Auschwitz[15]—whereas others see this precedent
among the conquistadors in Mexico and Peru, the "Afro-
American laboratory" (Georges Bensoussan), Leopold
II's dastardly seizure of the Congo, the colonization of
Australia by British convicts, or General von Trotha's massacre of the Herreros in Namibia in 1904? Any old butchery in history, from the Albigensians to the Vendéens, including the devastation of the Palatinate by Louis XIV's
armies and the Thirty Years' War in Bohemia, can prefigure in its own way the Wehrmacht's campaigns and their
cortege of horrors in Europe and the USSR—everything is
in everything. We see the advantage that a government in
need of legitimation can draw from such allegations: like
President Bouteflika of Algeria, taking advantage of the
commemoration of the repression in Sétif on May 8, 1945,
which resulted in several thousand fatalities, to accuse
Paris of genocide during the war for independence, referring to the "ovens analogous to the Nazis' crematories" in

[15] Le Cour Grandmaison, *Coloniser, exterminer*, p. 171. On this subject, see
the instructive article by Pierre Vidal-Naquet and Gilbert Meynier, "Com-
ment faire l'histoire des crimes coloniaux?": "More or less assimilating the
colonial system to an anticipation of the Third Reich, and even to a 'disquieting precedent' of Auschwitz, is an enterprise hardly more fraudulent
than the equation by the Algerian Ministry of Former Muhajadin on May 6,
2005, of colonial repression with the crematoria in Auschwitz and Nazism.
In Algeria there was neither a deliberately conceived and executed plan of
extermination . . . nor a coherent project of genocide. The Vichy government's law regarding the status of the Jews was attached, far more firmly
than the code regarding Algerian natives, to the biological delusion: it was a
Franco-French phenomenon distinct from the ordinary discrimination with
regard to third parties outside continental France" (*Esprit*, December 2005,
p. 16).

which hundreds of Fellaghas were supposed to have been burned. Thus he grants himself an unlimited credibility in matters concerning continental France and waves away the atrocities committed by the Algerians themselves during their war of liberation, first with regard to Messali Hadj's Algerian National Movement (MNA), which was in competition with the FLN, and then with regard to the Harkis and Pieds-Noirs.[16] Also forgotten are the FLN's state dictatorship from 1962 on, the repression of the Kabyle movement, and the civil war that has been waged against the Islamic Salvation Front and the Armed Islamic Group since 1991, which has caused more than 100,000 deaths (even if this war, we recognize, has prevented the establishment of an Islamic Republic only an hour away from Marseilles by plane). He points an accusing finger at France, refers to a "genocide of Algerian identity" [sic] to avoid leading his regime and his country to examine their consciences and inquiring into the epidemic of violence that has struck his country (including the omnipresent use of torture by its security forces). Constantly claiming to be the victim of a crime against humanity is a way of telling everyone else: don't judge me! It amounts to

[16] In the journal *Hérodote* (no. 120, 2006), Bernard Alidières, a professor at Paris VIII, refers to France's "forgotten memories" of the Algerian war—the murders, liquidations, and settlings of scores among immigrant supporters of the FLN and the MNA in Maghrebin neighborhoods, at bus stops, and in cafes and factories between 1955 and 1962, episodes of violence that made a major contribution to the stereotype of the violent Arab in France. Benjamin Stora, speaking of the conflicts between the two rival components of Algerian nationalism that caused several thousand deaths, refers to "a ditch full of blood within immigrant groups." The Harkis were Muslim Algerians who fought alongside the French in the Algerian war and Pieds-Noirs were European colonists born in Algeria.

taking up permanent residence in the most impregnable position, that of the damned of the earth. As a rule, the acrimony of the formerly colonized peoples with regard to the home country depends on two factors: the degree of the occupation's harshness, and the strength or weakness of national feeling. Compare the relative serenity of Morocco concerning France with the bitterness Algerian officials continue to feel toward us: the conquest and the war of independence were in the latter case characterized by particular cruelty, but especially Algeria remains, forty years after the Évian Accords, a nation of uncertain individuality, whereas Moroccan monarchy guarantees the unity of the kingdom. In Algiers, anti-French feeling is still the ferment of the absent national unity: either identity is a collective project or it is a rejection, and thus a negative construction opposed to a demonized third party. But this demonization is precisely what prevents the country from surmounting its trauma and beginning to reflect on itself.

In the same way, assimilating triangular commerce to genocide, forgetting that the slave traders, as good utilitarians, had no interest in decimating their labor force and had to get it to the other side of the Atlantic in the best condition possible,[17] is once again a way of demanding maximum incrimination to one's own benefit: Nazism is supposed to have begun on the day that the white man, whether Portuguese, Spanish, or Dutch, set foot on the shores of Africa or America, sowing death, chaos, and destruction. It is as if the Third Reich had literally swallowed,

[17] Cf. Pétré-Grenouilleau, *Les Traites négrières*, p. 12.

one after the other, the centuries that preceded it, thus becoming the key to violent or atrocious phenomena that
occurred several centuries earlier. But one cannot truncate
or manipulate history just to please this or that minority.
All the despots and tyrants of Europe are not reducible
to Hitler, who is not a registered trademark. There is no
need to "Nazify" slavery to make it odious. People find it
hard to realize that barbarity is plural, that not all mass
crimes are genocides, that not all genocides resemble each
other, that there degrees and diversity in horror as well.
To refuse to see the gassing of the Jews and Gypsies between 1940 and 1945 as special cases of the slave trade or
colonialism is not to minimize the latter. They constitute
different categories of evil because it seems that in this domain human imagination knows no limits. The claim to
have priority: we were the first, we are hyperbolic Jews.[18]
In the hierarchy of martyrology, we are at the top of the
ladder. And the same people who contest the uniqueness

---

[18] For the historian Rosa Amelia Plumelle-Uribe, the Shoah was ultimately
only a misunderstanding among white people, who after the end of the
Second World War hastened to reconcile with each other at the expense of
Africans and Latin Americans, supporting, for example, apartheid in South
Africa or in Israel: "When I say that there are acts whose criminality has to
do with the identity of the victims, it is because these acts are considered
criminal when they are committed in Europe against Europeans, but change
their name and become more or less acceptable when they take place elsewhere and Europeans are no longer their victims" (*La Férocité blanche*, p.
291). Accusing Europeans of having made a selection among victims—good
Jewish victims, bad black, American Indian, or Palestinian victims—she
complains that three centuries of Euro-American barbarity directed at the
rest of the world counts less than twelve years of atrocities committed by
the Nazis in Europe. She attributes this to "the influence, often crushing, of
white supremacy on our unconscious" (p. 304). A strange racialist conclusion for someone who claims to be fighting the perverse effects of racism!

and singularity of the Shoah do it homage by seeking at all costs to align their tragedy with it. In this case, they limit themselves to forging a new sacred history: finding from Spartacus to our own time a single, unique figure of the Pariah whose history is to be written retrospectively on the basis of National Socialism. The great ordeal of the oppressed ever since the dawn of time must develop in the shadow of the swastika or be nothing at all.

The Twofold Colonial Nostalgia

On February 23, 2005, the French parliament, concerned to show the nation's sympathy with the people repatriated from Algeria, Pieds-Noirs and Harkis, passed a law recognizing "the positive work of our fellow citizens who lived in Algeria during the period of French presence there." Article 4 of this law states that "school programs in particular will recognize the positive role of the French presence overseas, notably in North Africa, and give the history and the sacrifice of the military combatants that came from this territory the eminent place they deserve." This law, apparently approved on the basis of clientelism and a certain indifference on the part of the opposition,[19] constitutes a double error: it promulgates, as in the ex-USSR, an official history written by the state, and it hands down from on high (but under pressure from the interested

[19] On the circumstances and the vote on this law, see, for example, Claude Liauzu and Gilles Manceron, *La Colonisation, la Loi, et l'Histoire* (Paris: Syllepse, 2005), pp. 23ff.

lobbies) an edifying history contrary to the facts, since none of the peoples colonized by Paris wished our tutelage to be prolonged. A year later, this calamitous article, which caused an uproar in the Antilles and in Algeria and also triggered a petition by historians for freedom of research and against memorial laws,[20] was suppressed by Jacques Chirac. But it also intervenes in a context of ideological revisionism in which everywhere the goal is only to break the "taboo" on colonialism, to reflect on the "colonial fracture" that is supposed to explain, for example, the fragile situation and marginalization of immigrants' children born in France. "Colonial fracture":[21] this extremely vague term, a gadget borrowed from Chirac's vocabulary, makes it possible to explain almost anything and draws its power from its false simplicity. Does it mean that France is still marked by its recent history? That amounts to stating the obvious. Does it mean that immigrants from our former colonies are badly treated, relegated to subaltern tasks? That employers and public authorities dream of importing them when they need them and sending them back when there isn't enough work? That is true in virtually all European countries, even those that have no imperial past. Are these migrants less well treated than the Tamils, the Chinese, the Pakistanis, the Filipinos, or even the Balts

---

[20] *Libération*, December 13, 2005. The historians were themselves divided regarding the necessity of maintaining or abolishing memorial laws, starting with the Gayssot law (1992), which punishes the crime of negationism.

[21] Pascal Blanchard, Nicolas Bancel, and Sandrine Lemaire, *La Fracture coloniale: la société française au prisme de l'héritage colonial* (Paris: La Découverte, 2005).

and Poles, all nationalities that we have not colonized?[22] Are they less well treated than the Gypsies in Romania, whose temporary buildings are regularly destroyed and whose networks are dismantled by the police? Isn't it instead France that has difficulty with its foreigners in general and opposes its protectionist system to all of them?

In truth, the trial of colonialism has been reopened not because it was ignored or repressed in the schools,[23] but because it provides clarity for all those who are nostalgic for the old divisions. Just as there are people who miss the Cold War, there are intellectuals who have never mentally

[22] An article in *Le Monde* (February 17, 2006) pointed out that Poles with university degrees were reduced to babysitting in Paris and that the French labor market remained closed to young people from Eastern Europe. Is this a colonial or Malthusian attitude protecting our workers?

[23] An inquiry carried out by the daily newspaper *Libération* (October 17, 2005) reveals that of six history textbooks consulted on the subject, three give an unvarnished account of the violent repression in Paris on October 17, 1961, in which several hundred Algerians were drowned in the Seine or beaten to death by French policemen. Another inquiry, this time by the *Nouvel Observateur* (December 8–14, 2005) and devoted to four textbooks used in the final years of high school, shows that the period of the colonies and slavery is extensively dealt with in history books, which paint a dark and critical picture of European domination. A third inquiry into this subject, carried out for *Le Monde* (December 25–26, 2005) by Philippe Bernard and Catherine Rollot, arrived at the same conclusion: "Not only does colonization figure in the curricula, but it occupies a considerable place in the textbooks, and thus, in theory, in classes. Far from transmitting a Manichean view of colonial conquest and its consequences, the courses, their iconography, and the texts that illustrate them offer a complex account in which the realities are questioned more than they are hammered in." (Quoted in Faes and Smith, *Noir et français*, pp. 332–33.) What one ought to demand of textbooks is that they take into account the state of research at a given point and the controversies among historians, not that they dispense moral lessons. Valérie Esclangon-Morin complains that people want to write colonial history in the form of a positive/negative table, congealing it into a stereotype ("Quelle histoire de la colonisation française?" in Liauzu and Manceron, *La Colonisation*, pp. 99ff.)

accepted the independence of territories that used to be
under French administration. Anticolonialism serves as a
substitute for Marxism for a whole segment of the Left that
no longer knows how to understand the world. Since the
idea of the nation includes all the defects of Western domination—expansionist, it falls into the sin of imperialism;
confined to its own borders, it falls into the sin of chauvinism and racism—this Left has to produce, relying heav-
ily on artifices, the image of a France that is xenophobic
because it is France, that is, branded with a criminal past.
The wretched situation of Maghrebins and blacks is supposed to be explained by "the persistence and application
of colonial schemas to certain categories of the population (categories that are real or constructed), mainly those
who have come from the former French empire."[24] "Our
parents and grandparents have been enslaved," states the
Appel des Indigènes, published by several collectives during the winter of 2005 and supported by various left-wing
figures close to Islamist milieus: "As daughters and sons of
immigrants, we are . . . engaged in the struggle against the
oppression and discrimination produced by the postcolonial Republic. . . . We have to put an end to institutions
that reduce to subhuman status people who have come
out of colonization." According to these new vulgates, social problems are first of all ethnic problems (note the rhetorical similarity to the discourse of the Front National),
and the low-cost housing projects in the suburbs where

---

[24] Blanchard, Bancel, and Lemaire, *La Fracture coloniale*, pp. 24–25.

many immigrants live are nothing other than our new do-
minions, in which the inhabitants are silenced and kept
in a system of institutional racism.[25] Paris is supposed to
steal from the projects, exploit their wealth, and conduct a
violent policy of despoiling them! Let us recall that others
have tried to make these areas the equivalent of the occupied territories in Palestine, a Gaza Strip or a West Bank
of their own around Lyons, Toulouse, or Paris. So now the
French have become colonists at home, and the hexagon
will have to be taken from them! Instead of admitting
that the French system discourages initiative and effort,
that an unemployment rate of 40 percent among young
people in the projects, the absence of qualifications and
interfamilial solidarity, and the omnipresence of gangs
that rule the projects and regularly shake down the inhabitants of the apartment blocks there make their situation
catastrophic, a fantastic genealogy is invented, and areas
like Les Minguettes and La Courneuve are seen as if they
were the Aurès mountains of Algeria or the high plateaus
of Tonkin. Here we are in a kind of spatio-temporal tele-
scoping, a superposition of continents and eras in which
everything is mixed up, Seine-Saint-Denis with South
African townships, Clichy with Gaza, Bobigny with the
slave trade. According to his inclinations, everyone can
live in the virtual country of slavery or colonialism, which

[25] "In France today, individuals in 'sensitive neighborhoods' are reduced
to silence on the political level, kept in a very strong economic dependency,
and socially and culturally dominated by a veritable system of the institu-
tionalization of racism and colonial relationships." Didier Lapeyronnie, in
ibid., p. 120.

have become vague concepts, temporary habitats, that one enters in order to express one's anger, one's disgust.[26] The situation in the projects has to do with rejection, with territorial separation, not with the subordination to commercial ends that was the peculiar feature of empires. The colonists held a country and did not abandon it; they did not make of it a "lost territory of the Republic." When a government abandons part of its citizens—the unemployed, those whose right to support has run out, poor people, subproletarians, people living on welfare— we don't say that it colonizes them, we say that it neglects them.[27] Just as for half a century we have been bombarded by supporters of resistance—that is, individuals born after 1945 who dream of cleansing themselves of the affront of collaborationism by fighting "fascism," we see coming back a generation of Third Worldists who are resuming the battles for liberation half a century after the countries

[26] Thus when a singer from Côte d'Ivoire, Alpha Blondy, says regarding the law on selective immigration passed by the parliament on May 18, 2006: "This notion of selective immigration takes us back to the time of slavery, when the traders chose the most vigorous, those who had the best teeth, to bring them to the West" (AFP, May 14, 2006), he is mixing at least three periods: the present, the era of apartheid in South Africa, and that of the slave trade. In his excessiveness, he simply forgets that slavery was forced, that men and women were sold against their will, whereas no one compels Africans to emigrate to France.

[27] Accusing the Left of victimizing the children of immigrants, Béatrice Giblin emphasizes that facing the natives, there are also the "Indigents" of the Republic, a Franco-French proletariat, for example in the terraced miners' houses in the old mining area in Nord-Pas-de-Calais or in certain areas of the rural world, a whole population that is too crushed by poverty to remind politicians of their existence or to set fire to the housing projects. Béatrice Giblin, "Fracture sociale ou fracture nationale?" *Hérodote*, no. 120 (2006), pp. 77ff.

of the South won their independence and are feverishly rehearsing their anticolonialist catechism and announcing that they are going to liberate "9-3."[28] They make one think of those Japanese soldiers scattered around the Pacific islands who at the end of the twentieth century still didn't know that the Second World War was over. It is a vocation to be a hero once the fighting is over; it gives you the luster of being a sniper without exposing you to the slightest danger. But a historian cannot allow ideology—even the most generous—to dictate his craft without reducing his discipline to the rank of simple propaganda.

However, it is regrettable that it is necessary to recall such a simple matter. Decolonization happened. Very imperfectly, no doubt, but France finally put an end to colonization. If it wants to forget this period or is reluctant to remember it, that is because in this area amnesia is the counterpart of detachment. Will someone bring up in this connection "Françafrique," its scandals and its networks of secret agents, its dirty tricks borne by de Gaulle, Giscard, Mitterand, and Chirac? It was primarily a relationship of "mutual corruption" (Achille Mbembe) in which Paris and a few African heads of state held each other by their goatees; today, it is about to end, as is shown by the sad quagmire in Côte d'Ivoire. How can one fail to see that the real danger today is not expansion but abandonment, pure and simple? According to the economist Paul Bairoch's brusque formulation, "The West doesn't need the Third

---

[28] That is, department no. 93, Seine-Saint-Denis, where many impoverished North Africans live.

World, which is bad news for the Third World."[29] In short, to the misfortune of being exploited corresponds the still greater misfortune of no longer being exploitable, of being abandoned. What threatens many deprived countries in the South is not the invasion of the capitalist octopus, but the inverse: no longer interesting either investors or large economic groups, being excluded from global circuits. Nothing would be worse than a unilateral withdrawal, a rupture of ties forged over the centuries. It is to Europe that France must bequeath its African preserve, since Europe alone is able to deal with this continent, so as to weave coherent relationships and not to burn bridges.

Colonialism has thus become a portmanteau word that no longer designates a specific historical process but everything that is rejected—the Republican ideal, the French model, secularism, the influence of the multinationals, and who knows what else? It is true that a small fraction of those repatriated from Algeria long for French Algeria; but a large fraction of the intellectual Left longs for it no less, mourning for the revolutionary romanticism and the political energy of that period. For the Left that

[29] Paul Bairoch, *Mythes et paradoxes de l'histoire économique* (Paris: La Découverte, 1994), quoted in Daniel Cohen, *La Mondialisation et ses ennemis* (Paris: Grasset, 2004), p. 11. To the false idea according to which the West got rich by pillaging the Third World, Daniel Cohen opposes two facts: the colonial powers had a slower economic growth than noncolonial powers, and the countries of the North did not develop as a result of the exploitation raw materials imported from poor countries because the rich countries had long produced these raw materials. (Ibid., pp. 61–62.) The standard work on this subject is Jacques Marseille, *Empire colonial et capitalisme français* (1984; rpt. Paris: Albin Michel, 2005).

sees the confrontation between rich and poor in terms of debts and credits, which is simultaneously whining and compassionate, immigration, instead of being an opportunity for those who left and for the country they went to, is supposed to be a simple restitution: France (or Holland, Britain, or Spain) is said to be paying its debts to Africa by receiving its children. Europe owes the latter everything: housing, healthcare, education, decent salaries, immediate consideration, and especially respect for their identity. Before they have even set foot on our soil they have legal claims and have come to be reimbursed. "Anyway, the real victory will come when France accepts you even if you don't play soccer," says a strange ad produced by the Catholic Committee against Hunger and for Development, showing the photo of a boy playing with a ball in an African village at the time of the soccer World Cup in 2006.[30] We might wonder if this Christian and somewhat paternalistic view of the immigrant is not itself imbued with a colonial perspective in reverse, which consists in seeing the home country as eternally in debt to its former possessions.[31] (If immigration is not selective, it must therefore be passively undergone, accepted as an ineluctable phenomenon, a command issued by Providence;

[30] Comité catholique contre la faim et pour le développement, *Le Monde*, July 11, 2006.

[31] On the fact that immigration policies do not derive from the colonial past but follow from other sources of cultural legitimation, see the American researcher Erik Bleich's study of the integration of immigrants in France and Great Britain. "Immigrants from the former colonies are treated in the same way as other foreigners, with the same rights and the same abuses." "Des colonies à la métropole," in Weil and Dufoix, *L'Esclavage*, pp. 437ff.

it is curious to hear Socialist leaders praise a hands-off policy, erecting fatalism into a progressive slogan.) To cut the umbilical cord is to cease to argue in terms of debt and dependency; it is to privilege partnership over an affective or resentful relationship, which excludes neither solidarity nor responsibilities. There may be a second, mental revolution to be carried out on both sides, between Paris and the various African capitals, which will be no less arduous than the first one. As for the adjectives "decolonized" or "postcolonial," they have the defect of still indicating a relationship of subordination with the former system, confusing rupture with consequence, secession with continuity. One has to feel very sure of oneself to say, as did the president of the People's Republic of China on welcoming Mrs. Thatcher in 1985: "The British occupation awakened China from its immemorial slumber," or to emphasize, as did the Indian prime minister Manmohan Singh on receiving an honorary doctorate from Oxford on July 8, 2005, the positive aspects of the British Empire. Although India was later to combat the Empire, Singh said, it also had to recognize its "beneficial consequences." The past is not forgotten, it is quietly put in its place, digested.[32] These great nations—favored, it is true by their population, their power, and the very high level of their elites—have simply become the masters of their own destiny.

---

[32] As Jean-Luc Racine puts it in "L'Inde émergente ou la sortie des temps postcoloniaux," *Hérodote*, no. 120, pp. 28ff. For Racine, India has entered its "postcolonial phase," and this is a sign of genuine national maturity.

Now We Have an Enemy!

Hannah Arendt speaks somewhere of the "terrible distance that separates us from our beginnings," especially in democracies, which are always inclined to abandon their principles, to corrupt their ideals. For this degradation there is a dreadful remedy: the presence of a good enemy who terrorizes us as much as he mobilizes us, reminds us that we can lose everything, that life cannot be reduced to tranquil personal development. "O you who are my brothers because I have an enemy," Paul Éluard said. Combining fanaticism and technology, our current enemy, Islamist terrorism, strikes at random, in cities, in public places, with the blindness of a natural phenomenon. It is a punishment without demands, without designated guilty parties, without any goal other than to kill and destroy. This terror, which is present everywhere and locatable nowhere, can paralyze the spirit, lead it to adopt a policy of capitulation. It can also sharpen our understanding of adversity, lead us to distinguish what has to do with military and political operations from what has to do with the war of ideas. Part of Islam is becoming radical not because it is moving away from us but, on the contrary, because it is coming closer to the West: in this antagonism there is no clash of civilizations but rather a violent convergence. The most extreme Islamists, as we know, are emerging from university science departments and belong, in general, to the well-off classes. A pathology of imitation and not of otherness.

As Nietzsche saw, the quest for purity of faith can be the flipside of skepticism or despair. Islam, in its fundamentalist version, has the main advantage of forcing us to re-evaluate everything we take for granted: secularism, the equality of men and women, the democratic system of government, freedom of expression, tolerance. It forces us, especially in France, to reconsider religion, to understand the phenomenon of belief, because what is sacred to us here in Europe is desacralization. A return to the great debates of the Enlightenment. Everything that seemed to go without saying has to be rethought because of the objections of religious believers, theologians, and imams determined not to concede anything to our permissive societies. These objections made to our certainties should not be waved away. Even if there is no doubt that Islamist radicalism will someday be overcome—but at the price of what suffering, of how many hundreds of thousands of dead?—let us agree that we now have an enemy and that this helps us remain vigilant, in a state of alert. Here we can truly say with Thucydides: "Your hostility does us less harm than your friendship." The adversary puts us in the contradictory position of wanting to defeat him and wanting to preserve him in order to retain the energy he instills in us. He is at once detestable and desirable.

CHAPTER SIX

Listen to My Suffering

It's hard being black. You ever been black?

I was black once—when I was poor.

—LARRY HOLMES

former heavyweight boxing champion

The fact that in France a certain number of black or Maghrebin citizens would like to redefine their contract with the Republic because they feel unloved or underrepresented is proof of the Republic's health. That they want to be seen as full-fledged French citizens, not a separate group within the body politic, that they denounce discrimination on the basis of appearance or family name, that they exclaim that *leur couleur est leur douleur*, as a Moroccan worker expressed it on television, is both just and legitimate. France—and this is both its greatness and its limitation—postulates the abstraction of the Citizen and privileges the right to resemblance over the right to difference: but it too often forgets that resemblance also applies to those who differ from us, men and women from other places, with other skin colors, or other religions, who have the right to enter the magic circle of the similar. In *The Invisible Man* (1952), Ralph Ellison used an allegory to draw attention to the invisibility of his black compatriots in the United States, their skin color making them interchangeable and depriving them of their individual identity. In France, too many minorities feel that they are socially dead, imperceptible because they are too visible, concealed by their ostentation, doomed to remain forever "pre-someones" (Évelyne Kestenberg).

On Victimization as a Career

What counts is knowing what mobilizes these collectivities: scorn for their equal rights, or an outrage so deep that it puts them in a state of unlimited indebtedness? Claiming a place in the public sphere by reappropriating the past, knowing and communicating, for example, the history of the Algerians, Moroccans, and Senegalese who died for France and were used as cannon fodder in our European wars (see Rachid Bouchared's film *Indigènes*), is part of a legitimate process of self-revaluation for their children and grandchildren. Symbolic recognition by the highest state authorities can complete this process, and France would be wrong to conceal the Arab-African side of its identity.[1] But there is also the danger of transforming these groups' suffering into a kind of sanctuary, if necessary by embodying it in a law, of making it an impenetrable bastion. Heirs: traditionally that term referred to the children from good families who enjoyed a large fortune and a good education. Now the word refers to the transmission of a new patrician value: suffering, which raises us to an unprecedented aristocratic order. We are all heirs on both sides of the same barrier, perpetuating a distinction or a defect that marks us forever. We no longer create our own lives, we repeat the injuries of former times. What victimist thought resuscitates is the old religious category of the curse. How then can we avoid transforming ourselves into lobbies of professional sufferers, competing with others for market share and the martyr's crown? Just as there are imaginary Jews, there are imaginary slaves and colonized peoples who want to

---

[1] In Toulon on August 15, 2004, on the occasion of the sixtieth anniversary of the Allied landing in Provence, Jacques Chirac paid homage to the contribution made by Maghrebins and Africans to the liberation of France.

drape themselves in an accursed legend and thereby win additional esteem. Thus would be reconstituted the great fraternity of the shipwrecked and defeated, confronted only by oppressors and torturers. Victimization would be a kind of savage positive discrimination, a way of giving oneself a free pass when all legal and political recourse have been exhausted. To call oneself a victim is to make oneself a candidate for exception; perhaps that is an indispensable stage that has to be passed through by a minority that is reconstructing itself and reconquering its dignity. But it is a two-edged blade. A feeling of belonging cannot be founded on a theatricalized misfortune, it has to be founded on a shared collective experience, a growing responsibility in public life, in the media, and in professions. Victimization does not produce a sectarian emphasis on difference, as supporters of the Republican model fear, it constructs conglomerates of plaintiffs, it forges ex nihilo an absent community. This allocation of prestige to the "defeated" or those who feel themselves to be defeated is ambiguous. It is a mistake to believe that making schoolchildren feel guilty in accord with the principle "your ancestors enslaved mine" will make them like the idea of human diversity any better or will seem to them anything more than a theatrical artifice.[2] Just imagine little blond, brunette, or curly-headed kids coming up to each other on the playground and introducing themselves

[2] That is what Sandrine Lemaire seems to think when she assigns to schools the role of tranquilizers that might, through a better teaching of history, "calm the tensions involved in certain inter-community cohabitations" (in *La Fracture coloniale*, p. 94). This is to confuse instruction with compassion.

as descendants of slaves, of colonized peoples, of slave-traders, of bandits, of peasants, of beggars! Why ask boys and girls to make themselves the contemporaries of crimes that may have been committed three centuries ago by unknown people in Nantes, Bordeaux, or La Rochelle, when they themselves are allergic to any idea of slavery? In short, whereas Europe has buried its age-old quarrels and reconciled its hereditary enemies, only the slave trade and imperialism are supposed to escape history, that is, distancing, and we are supposed constantly to inject rage and anger into them, repeating like a refrain Faulkner's famous phrase: "The past isn't dead, it isn't even past."

As a result, a veritable civil war between incompatible memories is beginning, making it impossible to establish a common narrative because there will always be groups that, because of their beliefs or sufferings, will not recognize themselves in it.[3] Unless there is a federating national or supranational narrative that brings all the diverse components of a country together and gives them a common impulse, the country becomes an agglomeration of black, North African, Gypsy, Antillese, Corsican, gay, etc. tribes unified by their mutual dissensions and relying on the state only as a simple mediating authority. Then identity ceases to coincide with citizenship; it is in fact what makes

[3] The Obin report, submitted to Education Minister François Fillon in February 2005, explained the difficulties encountered by teachers when speaking of the philosophers of the Enlightenment ("Rousseau is contrary to my religion"), studying Molière's *Tartuffe*, reading *Madame Bovary*, the story of an unfaithful wife, promoting secularism, referring to the building of cathedrals, examining the plan of a Byzantine church, admitting the existence of pre-Islamic religions, talking about anti-Semitic persecutions, and so on.

citizenship impossible. The French or British model may be in difficulty, but everywhere in Europe there is, as we have seen, a disqualification of the idea of the nation that renders absurd even the concept of integration. The latter is reduced to two complementary models. The free-market model makes settlement in a country equivalent to a labor contract that can be renewed or canceled in accord with the law of supply and demand. The Third World or Christian model of hospitality requires us to welcome anyone who comes to our country, without demanding anything of him or her, in an act of pure oblation. If there are no longer any patriots or natives, there are no longer any foreigners, either, only well-off people who have a duty to help their less well-off neighbors. Only the welfare state, through the allocations it provides us, reminds us that we are still in a certain place, with a certain government. What is lacking is a symbolic adherence to a spiritual principle, the result of a singular history, and a freely accepted, voluntary association with a specific national community, with all that presupposes in the way of learning the language and being introduced to that community's peculiar culture. It is not enough to regularize the status of thousands of immigrants, to provide them with a life and suitable work. In addition, if they want to stay in Europe, we must make them true Europeans—Spaniards, French, Italians—and this presupposes a political society sure of itself and of its values that can arrange, for example, a formal welcoming ceremony for newcomers. We blame great nations, often rightly, for their failures to absorb immigrants. But we forget that there is also a despotism on the part of the minorities, who resist assimilation if it is not accompanied by extraterritorial status.[4]

Still more serious is the fact that under cover of respecting cultural or religious differences (the basic credo of multiculturalism), individuals are locked into an ethnic or racial definition, cast back into the trap from which we were trying to free them. Their good progressive friends set blacks and Arabs, forever prisoners of their history, back into the context of their former domination and subject them to ethnic chauvinism. As during the colonial era, they are put under house arrest in their skins, in their origins. By a perverse dialectic, the prejudices that were to be eradicated are reinforced: we can no longer see others as equals but must see them as inferiors, victims of perpetual oppression whose past ordeals interest us more than their present merits. (The whole problem with "prides"—gay, bi, trans, Breton, black, etc.—which generally proceed from stigmatized categories, is that they imply the contrary of what they say: that one might be ashamed of what one is. It is revelatory that this expression, which comes from the politics of identity, has

---

[4] According to an ICM poll published on February 19, 2006, by the *Sunday Telegraph*, 40 percent of the Muslims in Great Britain want to establish Sharia there. Thinking that the Jewish community has too much influence on diplomacy, they oppose the war on terrorism and feel uncomfortable in British society. One out of five persons questioned expressed sympathy with the motives of the suicide bombers who participated in the attacks in London on July 7, 2005, even if 96 percent of the people polled condemned these terrorist attacks. Another, even more troubling poll published by the *London Times* in early July 2006 showed that 13 percent of British Muslims considered the London suicide bombers to be martyrs, while 7 percent thought suicide attacks on civilians in Great Britain were justified under certain circumstances.

become a slogan for everyone. One should be proud, not of what one is and that is not up to us, but of what one does.) To Europeans, African Americans seem first of all to be American citizens, with all that implies on the cultural, linguistic, and economic levels.[5] In everyday life I do not encounter "Jews," "blacks," or "Arabs," which are just abstract categories; I encounter distinct persons, whom I like or don't like, and to whom I am bound by precise affinities, but whose roots, whose pale or colored skins, and whose religious convictions play only a secondary role in my judgment of them. Individuals exist as such only when their singularity is more important than their nationality, the color of their skin, or their membership in a group.

The predominance of the racial over the social, of the ethnic over the political, of the minority over the norm, of memory over history, is contemporary with the explosion of the trial as the total tragedy of modernity, with its three principal actors: the claimants, the judge, and the lawyer. Here we are no longer in the classical power relationship, in a battle to arrive at a result, but in a court where the outcome depends on the adverse parties' rhetorical cleverness and on the influence of opinion. This tribunal has become the truth of all struggles, including the class struggle, which is henceforth subject to its jurisdiction. It even enrolls the

[5] When a group of African Americans was invited by the government of Ghana to come and rediscover their roots, they were shocked to be called "whites" by the natives. Their economic prosperity and purchasing power "whitened" them for the people of Ghana. The latter envied them because they lived in the United States and were trying to go there themselves; they could not understand why the Americans wanted to come back to Africa. *New York Times*, December 27, 2005.

state under its banner; it is the sole common denominator in a divided world. In the United States, lawyers investigate companies suspected of having had ties with slavery a century and a half earlier; in France, the national railway company, SNCF, is taken to court for its supposed complicity with the Nazi death machine (SNCF trains were used to transport Jews to the camps). Tomorrow, the shipping companies that participated in the slave trade will be attacked. We will reawaken the religious wars of the sixteenth and seventeenth centuries, set Orthodox, Protestant, and Catholic Christians against one another, and mine the endless galleries of the past in order to put them in the service of our quibbling passions. All punishment being the consequence of an offense, we will need solvent scapegoats whose degree of noxiousness can be calculated in dollars and cents. The century that is beginning will be one of generalized litigation: suits involving the repair and restitution of works of art will multiply exponentially; if necessary, all the museums will be emptied to send back every painting, every sculpture and bas-relief, to its original owners, the notion of imprescriptibility being extended to all domains. Statutes of limitation have been abolished. Will the working class someday demand that capitalism pay damages and interest for its shameless exploitation of workers over two centuries? As soon as we acquire the status of legal claimants, we immediately acquire that of injured parties as well. *Each of us is given at birth a portfolio of grievances to exploit.* History as a whole owes us a debt which we demand be immediately repaid. Today, we combine romanticism with suffering; we form a new elite caste, with an absolute allergy to pain, the ideal being to acquire the title of pariah without having actually endured anything. The slightest adversity we encounter is a scandal that has to be indemnified. To set oneself up as a victim is to give oneself a twofold power to accuse and demand, to cast opprobrium on others and to beg. And since each of us has in our family tree at least person who was hanged, one proletarian, one victim of persecution, we will go back as far as the Middle Ages if that is what it takes to demand justice. Classical political combat trained warlike men and women who were proud of their conquests, whereas contemporary legal combat produces chronic malcontents. It is not clear that this represents progress.

Protect Minorities or Emancipate the Individual?

All the ambiguity of multiculturalism proceeds from the fact that with the best intentions, it imprisons men, women, and children in a way of life and in traditions from which they often aspire to free themselves. The politics of identity in fact reaffirm difference at the very moment when we are trying to establish equality, and lead, in the name of antiracism, back to the old commitments connected with race or ethnicity. The protection of the rights of minorities is also the right, for each individual belonging to these minorities, to withdraw from them without harm because he is indifferent to them or no longer feels clan or familial solidarities, and to forge a new destiny that is specific to him, without having to reproduce what his parents bequeathed him. It is therefore the right to exist as a private individual, to become someone else who does not derive from his roots but imprints on his life the meaning he wants to give it. What would Republican emancipation mean? Social promotion and forgetting biological and cultural determinisms: getting blacks and Arabs out of the subaltern roles and arduous tasks to which they are too often limited. Freeing them from the stereotypes that reduce them to being athletes, bouncers, manual laborers, etc. Making them, if necessary by deliberate correction of inequalities, visible in the public sphere, present at all levels of society, in business, the media, medicine, politics—in short, making them citizens in the fullest sense of the term (when will we see in France a Colin Powell, a Condoleezza Rice, or a Barack Obama rise to high office?). European citizenship has the immense advantage of conjoining the particular and the universal, of authorizing the individual's full development in twenty-seven countries linked by a single body of law. We can now accumulate self-definitions instead of excluding one to the benefit of another (one can, for instance, be Parisian, French, and European). European states are no longer oppressive but benevolent: the possibility of going to live or study in London, Amsterdam, Barcelona, Bologna, Krakow, Prague, or Budapest offers an extraordinary spiritual broadening in comparison to which a minority identity seems pathetically stunted.

Minorities, in proportion to the wrongs that have been inflicted on them, have acquired a prerogative that used to be peculiar to the bourgeoisie: unmitigated egoism and the pleasure of self-satisfaction. They noisily proclaim their personalities, take pride in being what they are, practice self-celebration, recognize no defect in themselves, authorize no challenge, and are even sometimes exempted from the common laws (in the United States, gay men and women cannot, except in rare cases, be accused of sexual harassment: the free expression of their libido is always innocent). We have transferred to minorities the privileges forbidden to the dominant classes and to nations. Moreover, a minority, whether ethnic, religious, sexual, or regional, is nothing more than that: a small nation restored to its angelism, cleansed of original sin, in which the most excessive chauvinism is only the expression of a legitimate self-esteem. On the pretext of celebrating the idea of diversity, we are at the same time separating people and making them unequal because some people, by the very fact that they exist, enjoy advantages that are forbidden to others. As a result, marginalities have a discipline that is no less severe than the other one, and a micro-nationalism that is just as jingoistic. Pressure to join in ethnic, racial, or religious solidarity and the denunciation of traitors, called "bougnoules" or "macaques" in the service of the dominant group,[6] serve to keep potentially recalcitrant members in line and restrain their aspirations to freedom. Every time a Western country has tried to create a special legal code for minorities, it has been members of those minorities, usually women, who have protested.

[6] In France, Tribu K, a small Black supremacist group that is also anti-Semitic, claims descent from the Pharaohs, asserts the racial superiority of Africans over the rest of the world, and denounces, essentially targeting SOS Racism, "all the macacas of Judeo-black friendship."

For example, Canada's generous provisions intended to allow Muslims to be judged in accord with Muslim law were
seen as a regression, a new confinement.[7] How can we not
be extremely distrustful of this mystique of alterity that is
now developing alongside the mystique of respect (whose
etymological meaning is "look at from a distance")? This
stranger who is close to me is not another version of myself;
he shines in his distant and inalterable splendor because
he has not been soiled by modernity. Multiculturalism
may ultimately be nothing more than that: a legal apartheid in which we find the wealthy once again explaining
tenderly to the poor that money won't make them happy:
let us shoulder the burden of freedom, of inventing ourselves, of the equality of men and women; you have the
joys of custom, forced marriages, the veil, polygamy, and
clitoridectomy. The members of these little congregations
then become museum pieces, the inhabitants of a reserva-
tion whom we want to preserve from the "calamities" of
progress and civilization. Some communities in Italy are
considering reserving beaches for Muslim women so that
they can swim without being seen by men. You'd think

---

[7] The Canadian province of Ontario attempted to accord religious tribu-
nals the right to decide cases regarding inheritances and family matters. A
Canadian woman of Iranian origin led the opposition to prevent this imposition of Sharia and to allow all citizens, without distinction of religion or
gender, to remain under the general legal system. In Germany Jutta Limbach, a former president of the Federal Constitutional Court and member
of the Social Democratic Party, proposed the creation of a minority status
in the German constitution, authorizing, for example, Muslim girls to be
excused from gymnastics at school. The reaction came from two women,
Germans of Turkish extraction, Necla Kelek and Seyran Ates, who empha-
sized the potential abuses of such a status: forced marriage, legal inferiority
of women, etc.

we'd returned to the time of segregation in the southern United States. In other words, we have to wage a double battle: protecting minorities from discrimination (favoring, for example, teaching regional languages and cultures, adapting the school calendar to religious holidays), and protecting private individuals from the intimidation that their birth communities may practice on them.

Victimization may be an ephemeral salve, but it is also an additional humiliation, a second servitude on top of the first one. No argument can contradict an individual's or a group's certainty that they are cursed, injured in their deepest interests. At least we should not maintain this feeling by means of a whole rhetoric of commiseration, not keep providing the injured with arguments that accentuate their distress. For example, in April 2001 France created a state secretary's office for victims, which is supposed to deal with "the memory of past and present victims, and also with potential victims," and *that* opens up, one will have to admit, a very broad spectrum. On December 30 of the same year, a High Authority for fighting discrimination and for equality (Haute Autorité de lutte contre les discriminations et pour l'égalité), which is to defend all persons who have had to suffer because of "their origin, gender, physical appearance, family name, sexual orientation, handicap, age, religion, or opinion," was created. We see the danger: the creation of a clientele of unfortunate persons who did not know they were unfortunate but whom these provisions will stimulate. We are not thereby healing wounds but creating new ones. "I was unhappy, I didn't know it, the government convinced me of it."

Will we someday create a new ministry for the emotion-
ally distressed? We are diverting public power from its
traditional responsibilities and reducing it to the role of
a psychologist, a social worker, a consoler of the afflicted.[8] It is curious, furthermore, that in France Indochinese
immigrant communities take hardly any part in this generalized complaint and refuse to adopt a tearful attitude:
many of them, it is true, came to France to flee communist
regimes, but it may also be that Vietnamese, Laotians, and
Cambodians rely only on themselves and do not join in
the ambient wallowing in misery.

When a rapper who wants to emphasize "the injustice
felt by the sons of the damned" sings, "France is a whore,
fuck her till she can't take more, you have to treat her like
a slut, guy" (Monsieur R); or another group (Ministère
Amer) exclaims, "Living in France what luck, too bad your
mother didn't tell you about this fucking country, where
I want to shoot these chalk-faces 24/7, chalk-faces in high
places, who keep me from expressing myself"; or when
the group "Lunatic" shouts, "When I see France with its
legs spread, I ram in my cock, without using oil . . . and
dream of putting a bullet from my Glock in a cop's head,"
they may be taking advantage of a commercial niche,
but they are not making French citizenship more desirable. The depth of the disgust is such, the dimension of
the wrong so vast, that it makes adherence to the nation
impossible. Seduction through insult is a tortuous proce-
dure: belittling the object by which one wants to be loved,

[8] See Michel Richard, *La République compassionnelle* (Paris: Grasset,
2006).

in this case France, by showering it with invective may sometimes work with masochists. But any normal person will react to insults by running away or rejecting. Let us say it again: those who do not like blacks, Arabs, Indians, Asians, Jews, gays, liberated women, anyone who is hostile to the diversity of physiognomies and the plurality of ways of life, to the great mixture of our cities, should not live in France. They should not walk in the street, use mass transit, or go to a restaurant or a café. They should not live in New York, London, Amsterdam, Madrid, or Rome, either. They are in the wrong century, to use Trotsky's famous expression. Monochrome Europe, which was mostly white, is gone. But those who think that France is a nation whose past is ignoble and whose ideals are repugnant, who see it as a simply provider of services in which one has all rights and no duties, are dooming themselves to feel torn apart, to a veritable psychological crucifixion, unless they go elsewhere and find a climate better suited to them. All those French youths of distant immigrant origin who hate France but have nowhere to go, who boo, for example, when the national anthem is played at soccer games and wave Algerian flags, but who will never go back to Algeria—these youths make us think of dysfunctional marriages in which the partners hate each other but can't make up their minds to separate and end up cohabiting in mutual antipathy. We can only ask them to take themselves in hand, to undertake a self-reconciliation, and to transform their anger into political action, into collective improvement. One cannot go on living forever in a country that one detests without ending up detesting oneself.

Questions about Slavery

Isn't it astonishing that the first nations that abolished slavery, after having greatly profited by it, were also the only ones that are now the object of accusations and demands for reparations? In other words, the crime is attributed only to those who have repented of it—Europe and the United States—which lost, by the way, a million of its sons for this cause in the Civil War—and who have condemned this commerce in human beings as a barbarity. In France, the Taubira law of May 21, 2002, which seeks to define as a crime against humanity only the Western slave trade, participates in this partial interpretation of the phenomenon. Why is the West and the West alone blamed, whereas the Asian and African worlds, which have never publicly apologized for it, are exonerated of all responsibility? Because the former is rich and sensitive to moral arguments: it was in the name of these arguments that, first in Britain in 1807, and then in Denmark and France, the West yielded to the abolitionists who denounced as infamous the reduction of a category of human beings to the status of "animated tools" (Aristotle), of chattels. (For the record, the first Arab Muslim state to abolish slavery was Tunisia in 1846, but the measure was not enforced until the French arrived in 1881. The Ottoman Empire abolished slavery in the early twentieth century. The slave trade was declared illegal in Yemen and Saudi Arabia only in 1962, and in Mauritania in 1980.) There is still a taboo on mentioning that there were three slave trades, the Eastern one, which began in the seventh century (an estimated seventeen million captives); the African, which provided slaves for use both in Africa and abroad (fourteen million persons); and the Atlantic, which, in a shorter period of time, led to the deportation of almost eleven million men, women, and children. Any historian who dares to discuss this is running the risk of being accused of revisionism. It was the West and the West alone that developed the abolitionist idea before it was disseminated in black Africa and in East Asia.

We are waiting for the Arab Muslim world to make a public acknowledgment and apology for its role in the "hunt for black skins" and to look into its own racism (in Arabic the word *abid*, slave, became, from the eighth century on, more or less synonymous with black).[9] In 2000 the president of Bénin (formerly Dahomey) publicly apologized for West Africans' participation in the slave trade. We know the antagonism that opposes the peoples of the Caribbean to those of Africa, who are suspected of having sold them, as is shown by numerous expressions in everyday language. It was thus perfectly legitimate to establish a day for commemorating slavery because it is humanity as a whole that was stained by this ignominy. But this day should also be a day of joy because it commemorates humanity's collective exit from one of its most horrible sins. It is equally indispensable to teach the details of this "infamous traffic." Teaching must at least restitute the phenomenon in all its complexity. We can choose to ramble madly on about the "war declared on the black world" by the Zionist authorities (Dieudonné, speech given in Algiers on February 16, 2005), although article 1 of the *Code Noir* (the law regarding black slaves, 1685) specifically prohibited Jews, "the declared enemies of the Christian name,"[10] from participating in the trade and ordered that they be expelled from the islands where

[9] Cathérine Coquery-Vidrovitch, "Le Postulat de la supériorité blanche," in Ferro, *Livre noir*, p. 867.
[10] See Louis Sala-Molins, *Le Code Noir ou le Calvaire de Canaan* (Paris: PUF, rpt. 2005), pp. 92–93, and the author's commentary on article 1.

they had taken up residence. We can also prefer the fac-
tual truth in a domain that researchers tell us is still dis-
credited among historians. But then let all those involved
in the crime, from India to the Americas, be called before the bar, let the offense be known, explored in all its
ramifications. Do you want to honor the memory of those
who were deported and tortured? Then continue the abolitionists' battle, fight to free from their chains the twelve
to twenty million people who are still enslaved today by
forced labor and traffic in human beings. How strange
it is, the silence of our great consciences on this urgent
topic!

What Duty of Memory?

We too often forget that the expression "the duty of memory" was coined by Primo Levi when he called upon the
survivors of the camps to testify to overcome their contemporaries' incredulity.[11] Over the years, this injunction
has become a veritable cult urging everyone to piously
preserve the memory of past catastrophes. The respect
owed the dead has been transformed into an ethics of
vigilance: our conscience must remain on the lookout, be
ready at any time to prevent the return of the horror. But
this is a useless knowledge: the duty of memory has never
made us more lucid regarding current evil; it prevented
neither Cambodia nor Rwanda nor Bosnia nor Chechnya

[11] As Henry Rousso reminds us in his book of interviews with Philippe
Petit, *La Hantise du passé* (Paris: Textuel, 1998), p. 43.

nor Darfur. On the contrary, it can lend legitimacy to a paradoxical hardening of hearts: if a crime doesn't take exactly the form of the Shoah between 1942 and 1945, we turn up our noses at it, we disqualify it as not even genocidal. What ought to horrify us leaves us cold. A proof *a contrario*: historians, to sensitize us to the horrors of slavery or colonization, are forced, at the price of intricate contortions, to describe them in the language of the Holocaust itself. Only yesterday's dread can mobilize us now, and it gives us the right to set aside everything that is not it.

But the memory of old persecutions serves chiefly to open up wounds, to begin an endless prosecution of the West. In this case, what is called "the duty of memory" is usually the imposition of an official history in which the roles are assigned in advance, a coagulated knowledge that resembles propaganda, paralyzes research, and impedes investigation. The period of imperialism is frozen in an eternity of bitterness. As in Greek tragedy, the sins of the fathers are transmitted to the sons, interminably, the wages of sin have no limit, and the centuries form one long saga of reprisals and bloody torments. The duty of memory is brandished by some only in order to arouse the duty of penitence in others. We exalt less the pedagogical virtues of knowledge than the punitive virtues of accusation. *The contrary of memory is not forgetfulness, it is history*. A memory that is still hot is concerned with fidelity to oneself; it calls upon people to identify with each other as a group, whereas history, as a critical discipline, is concerned with what is true for everyone (Pierre Nora). It protects us from the sin of anachronism, situates events in a certain continuity, and forbids us to judge preceding centuries from the point of view of the present. Memory intimidates, condemns, blasts; history desacralizes, explains, details. One divides, the other reconciles. History broadens the context, offers us a complex understanding of the past, makes us the contemporaries of our most distant ancestors. It also forbids us to judge, demystifies the subjectivity of reminiscences, and avoids "the tyranny of official chronicles" (Claude Liauzu). There is something very beautiful in the idea of the *Thousand and One Nights*, according to which it is stories that protect us from death: so long as Scheherazade speaks, her execution is delayed. So long as we can transform the world into narratives, even to narrate our own worst misfortunes, we are still alive.

Erected into an instrument of politics, memory is always threatened by resentment. As in the former Yugoslavia, when Serbian nationalists referred to past sacrifices to justify their exactions, we are awakening the dead, the tortured, throwing them in the faces of the living, and shouting: you don't have the right to remain calm, ask forgiveness. Given that logic, there are only rats and saints. To recite the endless list of butcheries, deportations, and assassinations of which our fathers are said to be guilty is to open a bottomless chest from which revenge and rage can be drawn to make contemporaries pay for the crimes of their ancestors. *To dig up all the bodies is to dig up all the hatreds, to apply the* lex talionis *to long-past centuries.* For example, this diatribe delivered by a professor of political philosophy demanding reparations for slavery:

We have to pay reparations for everything which, in the crime concerned, can be weighed, measured, quantified legally. . . . Hours and days, months and years, decades and centuries of slavery can be quantified. In lands where there was slavery, the gap between the average life expectancy of slave-holding colonists, on the one hand, and that of slaves on the other, is quantifiable. The quantity of work provided by the slave can be weighed, and his share of the revenue from the economic miracle of the sugar industry and some other industries can be measured. How much is a day of work worth? How many millions of slaves . . . ? How many years stolen? All that adds up to how many millions of days, once the lifetimes of the slaves before they died of exhaustion, or beatings, or the cruelest punishments . . . are counted? All these data are quantifiable. It is necessary and sufficient that economic historians feed data into their computers. Which will spit out figures. And the monstrosity of the highest of them will frighten people. And the tiniest of the lower ones will nonetheless be revolting. . . . Let us insist. Let the law deal with it. And let it require proportionate reparations, knowing that these will still not erase the villainy of this utilitarian genocide whose present and future descendants will retain uninfringed the right . . . to manage memory as they see fit or as they can. . . . Who should make reparations? The Christian nations in exact proportion to the justifications they produced for this commerce and for this slow, genocidal extermination.[12]

Let us now compare this with what Frantz Fanon wrote in 1952, at a time when decolonization was far from complete:

> Blacks and whites who have refused to allow them-
> selves to be imprisoned in the substantialized Tower
> of the Past will cease to be alienated. . . . I am a man
> and it is the whole past of the world that I have to
> retell. I am not solely responsible for the revolt in
> Santo Domingo. . . . I do not want to sing this past at
> the expense of my present and my future. . . . Don't I
> have other things to do on this earth than avenge the
> blacks of the seventeenth century? . . . I don't have
> the right, as a man of color, to wish for the develop-
> ment in the White man of a culpability with regard
> to the past of my race. I have neither the right nor
> the duty to demand reparation for my domestic an-
> cestors. There is no Negro mission: there is no White
> Man's Burden. Am I going to ask the white man of
> today to assume responsibility for the slave traders
> of the seventeenth century? . . . I am not a slave of
> the slavery that dehumanized my ancestors.[13]

Memory has at least two uses: narcissistic macera-
tion that no reparation could calm because it has taken

---

[12] Sala-Molins, *Le Code Noir ou le Calvaire de Canaan*, pp. xi–xii.

[13] Frantz Fanon, *Peaux noirs, masques blancs* (Paris: Seuil, 1972), pp. 183, 186.

itself as its end, obliterating every more elevated moral perspective, and mobilization that inspires us, sensitizes us to injustices. In the first case an armed memory seeks targets for its vengeance, reignites tensions, and launches reprisals is triumphant. In the second case, memory keeps alive the source of indignation and increases our allergy to present-day infamy.

But history consists as much of collective forgetting as it does of memory; it abolishes the blood debts societies contract among themselves. If we had to continue the quarrels of our predecessors, if all peoples had to ruminate their respective grievances, the world would be given over to fire and blood. That is why there is something very profound in Ernest Renan's remark that "Someone who has to make history has to forget history." We have to abandon the idea of reparations for each and every past injury: the tortured, the defeated, the belittled will not be avenged, no financial compensation will bring them back to life.[14] What is owed them is the historical truth, not an insatiable desire for punishment on the part of their descendants. We cannot go on forever using suffering to make demands on the future; the time of prosecution has to come to an end after a few generations, once the biological duration has been respected, and to make room for the work of the researcher. There comes a time when we have to let the dead bury the dead, taking with them their dissensions and their woes. Focusing on what separates us rather than on what unites us is always

---

[14] We know what a passionate debate the question of German reparations payments has elicited in Israel; this is a proof that money, even in large quantities, is not enough to pay the debt. See Segev, *Le Septième Million*.

dangerous. Oblivion is what makes room for the living, for newcomers who want to wipe away the obligations of the past and not bear the burden of ancient resentments. It is a power of beginning again for future generations.

The best victory over the exterminators, torturers, and slave traders of yesterday is the coexistence that is now possible among peoples and ethnic groups that prejudices and mentalities previously declared to be incompatible, it is that formerly dominated people are now treated as equals and engaged in a collective adventure. In each of our nations, millions of people have to learn to live together with differing histories. Their ancestors killed each other for reasons that today seem obscure or repugnant. They can continue to mistrust each other, live alongside each other and compete in sad passions; or they can abandon vindictiveness in favor of a will to get along, as we see in certain exceptional moments. "What is good about soccer in France is that people celebrate French players without asking whether they are black or not. Just because they are French" (Lilian Thuram). The ideal would be to arrive at an indifference to color, ethnic group, and identity, seeing only talents, proper names, individual strengths, exceptional persons rather than individuals crammed into fixed categories. We are not there yet, not in Brazil and not in the United States, but these two great multiracial countries are showing the way. We should be working on enlarging the human family, not on sanctifying past sufferings, which is always degrading for those who complain about them. To accomplish this task, good will is not enough. We need a whole politics of friendship, of benevolent sympathy: we need a miracle.

Portrait of the Damned of the Earth
as Rebellious Consumers

In general, the low-cost housing projects on the outskirts of Western European cities are connected with two main narratives: that of the working classes and that of decolonization. An attempt is made to see in them an alliance of the workers' insurrection with the battle against imperialism. But the rioters in the projects in November 2005 in France, no matter how disinherited they are, were first of all children of television and the supermarket. What are they demanding? As one of them put it: "dough and chicks," not the proletarian revolution or the eradication of poverty, but a simple version of the commercial dream. Born French, they now want to become French, but they feel themselves impeded by an invisible screen behind which they see their compatriots succeeding, working, and amusing themselves without inviting them to join the party. The color of their skin, and especially their social origin and their address, constitute an insurmountable barrier. Not in school, unemployed, harassed by the police, wanting everything right now, like everyone in this individualist society, they have nothing to lose, they have no goal other than angrily expressing their hatred of the police, burning down daycare centers, supermarkets, schools, social security centers, and libraries in suicidal acts that seek to cut them off still more from the rest of the nation. They compete with other groups in destroying and vandalizing, compare photos of their exploits on their cell phones, and dream of being on the television news someday. Their rebellion is a form of negative integration, an initiation rite in which fighting the riot police takes the place of the impossible revolt against an absent or nonexistent father. France humiliated their parents and now ignores them, and their rage can also be interpreted as a cry of disappointed love, a way of saying: we're here, we exist.

It remains that this rage manifests a genuine antipathy to working-class culture when these young rioters, some of whom are no older than twelve or thirteen, attack drivers in buses, trains, and the subway, systematically vandalizing collective equipment, terrorizing the humble people and employees who live alongside them in the apartment blocks and see the only way they can get to work, their car, go up in smoke. Burning cars is not simply a matter of attacking a mythology cherished by the French, but also of completing the confinement forcing the inhabitants never to go out of their apartments, and expressing a refusal of mobility. (However, with a strange timidity, these arsonists never burn cars in wealthy neighborhoods, as if they had internalized their exclusion.) As the collective "Stop la Violence," encouraged by the Socialist Party, noted in 1998: "Crooks are the death of the neighborhoods." These areas are shaken down by bosses, dealers addicted to "business" who are running a whole underground criminal network (estimated by a student magazine as being worth millions of euros a year). The rage becomes doubtful when excited rioters wearing hoods like members of the Inquisition set fire to public transport vehicles, rob and lynch high school or university students in demonstrations, strike the weakest, women and the elderly, shoot real bullets at firemen and policemen, and show no remorse, draping themselves in an angelism of revolt. For the most violent, killing is no more than a game, death given or received just an accident. If there were a large fascist party in France, it is from the "black-white-Maghrebin" youth that it would recruit its shock troops. It is not surprising that the violence of the "caillera," to use the name these gangs give themselves, fascinates the media, show-biz, and so many intellectuals on the Left. It is by its brutality, its affiliation with major criminality, that the *Lumpen*, "the dregs of corrupt individuals of all classes," as Engels called them in 1870, addicted to the exploitation and control of immigrant populations, attracts sociologists, actors, film-makers, and journalists. Here we can say with Hannah Arendt, speaking of the rise of Nazism, that we have the same story of "high society falling in love with its own underworld." That is what the housing projects are like: not a foreign body in the Republic, but a magnifying mirror of French passions, a reserve of talent and energy, but also of potential barbarity—racism, anti-Semitism, machismo, homophobia, a receptacle for the plebeians' worst instincts. To extricate ourselves from this situation will be of no use without a mixture of determination and generosity. We have to repress the most hardened ruffians and treat the others in a brotherly way, getting them out of this cycle of failure and violence. If we don't, most of them will remain a lost generation, inevitably oscillating between prison, the mafias, and the Islamists.

CHAPTER SEVEN

Depression in Paradise: France, a Symptom and Caricature of Europe

If a people no longer has the strength or will

to maintain itself in the political sphere,

that is not the end of politics in the world.

It is only the end of a weak people.

—CARL SCHMITT

No power can destroy the spirit of a people,

either from the outside, or from the inside,

if it is not itself already lifeless, if it has not

already perished.

—G.W.F. HEGEL, *Reason in History*

There is a nation that embodies the illnesses of Europe to excess, and adds other, more specific ones: France. These days, it is not easy to be French, that is, heirs to a glorious past whose ups and down bring out our pettiness in contrast. France, which until 1989 took advantage of its position between the United States and the USSR, was the big loser in the West when the Berlin Wall came down. The reunification of Germany, with its eighty million inhabitants and its wealth, awakened our inferiority complex, which had been nourished by three wars—in two and a half of which it was defeated, if we consider that the First World War drained France dry. The French idea of civilization, although it persists in the domains of luxury and fashion, is falling behind the vitality of the Anglo-Saxon and Hispanic models, which offer another social contract, another relationship between the state and the world. The French, who used to be past masters in the art of overestimating themselves—de Gaulle succeeded in convincing us that we were one great group of *résistants*—suddenly find themselves facing the reality of their weakening, and tolerate it poorly.

A Universal Victim?

Because it is no longer first, France has concluded that it is nothing, and for the past decade it has indulged in self-denigration, fixated on its pain like a spoiled child. It once considered its language the natural idiom of the human race, and now it is able only to moan, brood, and lick its wounds, going over and over its disgraces. Everywhere rages a morose jubilation in self-deprecation, as if France inevitably went along with suffering. It is not certain rappers' cries of hatred for the Republic that are worrying—hatred has to come out, even in music—it is France's disgust with itself that is a matter of concern and gives these anathemas the ring of truth. We dislike ourselves much more than they reject us. A country so unsure of itself is incapable of arousing enthusiasm in its youth, whether native or immigrant. A land of plenty populated by sixty-three million depressed people, France is both the most visited country in the world because of its beauty and one of the biggest consumers of psychotropic drugs and tranquilizers. It is as if this country, which used to be the beacon of the world, were suddenly realizing that it no longer determines the rules of the game. Something has escaped it; it has grown old without regenerating itself. To put it crudely, France is no longer where it's happening. The center of gravity has shifted. France used to suffocate within borders that were too confining; now it suffers from dwarfism in a world that is too big for it.

Who is to blame? Others, of course. Everything that is going wrong in France is due to the malice of foreign powers. Brussels, globalization, Islam, American imperialism, who knows what else? Even the poor get into the act. And the former Third Worldists who used to weep over the fate of India and China cannot find words harsh enough to castigate these ex-damned of the Earth who dare, the dirty rats, to emerge from deprivation and compete with us, and even buy our companies. The more our international scope shrinks, the more foreigners become a source of concern: it is from them that all dangers come—delocalizations, mafias, and epidemics. Down with the outside world! The dominant fantasy in the political and intellectual arena is conspiracy: a single magical thought denounces the creators of the conspiracy against France. One word synthesizes this feeling of dread, a word that has become indecent, like fascism or pedophilia: liberalism. Liberalism is the source of all our ills. What this term means remains very mysterious: a doctrine of the limitation of state power, of the protection of the individual's rights, or an apology for the market, for free enterprise and competition? If there is a common idiom in France, a basic Esperanto, it is the way in which all camps without exception, and even the head of state, angrily reject this doctrine, which has been, however, brilliantly illustrated from Montesquieu to Raymond Aron. The aversion is twofold: in the heritage of 1789, liberty is left aside in favor of egalitarianism, which has important links with despotism, making everyone equal at the lowest level; the approval of the extreme Left and extreme Right is sought. In the name of this imperative, "envy, jealousy, impotent hatred" (Stendhal) triumph. This leads the far Left, in matters of social welfare, to demand the punishment of the favored rather than the improvement of everyone's condition. The rich have to be chastised: the poor will get a symbolic satisfaction out of it. This allergy to liberalism is then directed against the United States. It is our enemy—symbolically, that is, even if our two nations have never gone to war against each other.[1] Our execration of America keeps us dependent on it. Why is there such a relationship consisting of mimetic rivalry? Because for the past two centuries, both France and America have seen themselves as the messianic nation par excellence, devoted to spreading the values of civilization everywhere. To be French is always more or less to feel invested with a mission. "France," Charles Péguy said, "is not only the eldest daughter of the Church, it also has in the layperson a sort of singular parallel vocation, it is undeniably a sort of patron and witness (and often martyr) of freedom in the world." Valéry later added ironically: "Our particularity, as French people, is to believe that we are universal," a remark that echoes that of Montesquieu: "I am a man by necessity, but I am French only by accident."

However, this planetary ambition was always tempered by an isolationist reflex, by a nationalism of contraction. We have already mentioned that at the high point of colonialism, during the 1930s, attachment to the empire remained lukewarm, despite the success of the International Colonial Exposition held in 1931, and popular sentiment remained impermeable to government propaganda. Overseas France was more a matter of concern for the state and the elites, usually on the Left, and elicited no

---

[1] In April 2003 a poll showed that the French, by a small majority, wanted Saddam Hussein to defeat the forces of the Anglo-American coalition. France's diplomatic virulence at this time went far beyond a statement of pacifism, which was in itself justified.

massive civic enthusiasm.[2] It was the "colonial party" that led France into this venture, it alone knowing what it had in mind for the Republic:[3] the French were reluctant, or indifferent, imperialists. Forgetting that their country almost lost its soul in the dirty war in Algeria, they are still most affected by the two world wars. There are few peoples who could withstand the test of three foreign invasions in less than a century (1870, 1914–1918, 1940–1944): not a single family was spared, not a single consciousness escaped the shock. From Maupassant to Claude Simon, our whole literature bears witness to this stain. Whereas England has not experienced the moral corruption of a foreign occupation since the Norman invasion of the eleventh century (and is protected by being an island), France still has not recovered from these episodes and continues to see itself in the mirror of defeat and collaboration.

To suggest, as does the historian Benjamin Stora, that our country is vibrating with colonial nostalgia and has never accepted the independence of the countries of the Maghreb, is to misunderstand the profound nature of a Republic that lives today in a patriotism of retraction (as the rejection of the European Constitution in the 2005 referendum showed). The rapidity with which in the early 1960s France got over the loss of its empire, forgetting at

---

[2] Cf. Girardet, *L'Aventure coloniale de la France*, pp. 197–99. Marc Ferro himself refers to "a public opinion that was slow to become enthusiastic and to discover the virtues of the colonial empire." *Le Livre noir du colonialisme*, p. 855.

[3] Charles-Robert Ageron, *France coloniale ou parti colonial?* In ibid., pp. 297–98.

the same time a few hundred thousand Harkis and Pieds-
Noirs, and turned its attention to the European adventure
proves that the colonial enterprise was probably not so
dear to the hearts of the French as people say.[4] It is true
that there is a chauvinistic nostalgia for past grandeur, but
it is for an abstract grandeur for which we are not prepared
to pay anything. The fantasy that torments France in the
early twenty-first century is not expansion, it is separation.
It is a mistake to describe France as a power that dreams
of dominating: at best, it is a country that is in need of a
destiny and is trying to survive. The memory of the glories
of yesteryear is accompanied by a complete renunciation
of the mentalities that were the condition for those glories. What a surprise to see, in the fall of 2005, rioters in
the projects defending their areas against the intrusion of
the police and state services as if France was barricading
itself behind its borders to protect itself from the outside
world: an imitation of besieged populations holed up here
and there in their Gallic villages. Consider the immigration problem: by its attitude, simultaneously repressive
and permissive, the Republic has put itself in a position
to lose on all fronts. Its visa policy, which is restrictive and
touchy, discourages the best minds of Africa and Asia,
who allow themselves to be snatched up by universities in
North America and Britain. Ultimately, it welcomes only
the least qualified, who are employed in servile, thankless

[4] The historian Antoine Raybaud has even spoken in this connection of a
bereavement without mourning, an "archeology of oblivion." "Postcolonia-
lisme," *Dédale* (Spring 1997), pp. 87ff.

tasks, and its bureaucracy and police then carry on an ignoble guerrilla war against them. A double incoherence that shows both our short-sightedness and our pettiness. France—and this is its current tragedy—is detaching itself from Europe and the world, like a great old man who feels death approaching. If tomorrow the people of the Antilles, Réunion, Guiana, the Comoros, New Caledonia, or even Corsica were to demand by a strong majority vote their independence, a demand that would be quite legitimate, no one would go into the streets to prevent this divorce. Better to shed some ballast, better to avoid turmoil, than to redefine more equitable and more responsible ties with our overseas departments and territories.

It may be the happiness of existence in France that explains this lack of boldness; there are few countries where the art of living and the cultivation of pleasures have been developed as much as in ours. Comfortable on their territory, the French, at least until the 1980s, have never emigrated in large numbers, and they reject mobility even within France, content to be from a region, a province, or a village. Whether to cultivate our garden or spread all over the planet—for centuries that was our dilemma. Today, this turning inward is a constraint that is imposed on us by our small size and our loss of influence. It is true that life is never better than in a country in decline, when a people's fading vitality increases the attractiveness of its traditions. Since Mitterrand—this is perhaps the great legacy of the Left—France has specialized in the worldwide promotion of recreational activities: Paris-Plage,

the Fête de la Musique, Nuit Blanche, etc. These are so
many modern versions of the Roman bread and circuses.
To satisfy this insatiable desire for amusement, we have
even gone so far as to import foreign holidays—Hallow-
een and Gay Pride, for example. It will be recalled that
in 2003 the leader of the (Trotskyite) Ligue Communiste
Révolutionnaire, Olivier Besancenot, very seriously proposed the creation of a broad strike party: a marvelous
idea that would allow our children to be strikers without
ever having worked. France could, moreover, establish
programs to train people for work stoppages and demonstrations that it could sell all over the world, since we
know so well how to transform discontent into diversion.
Our experience in this area is incontestable. This status as
a seller of leisure activities, which is connected with our
classical competence in the domain of high fashion, per-
fume, and the restaurant business, guarantees us a secure
future. The cult of vacations, which has in France been
erected into a national religion, may reflect, beyond the
need for relaxation, the desire to take a long vacation from
the century, to reduce our connections with the world to
the area of distractions. Even if it fell still further, France
would remain what it already is in part: a magnificent museum and an amusement park for tourists, without peer
for wealthy vacationers looking for sculpted landscapes,
manicured meadows, and medieval villages full of flow-
ers. But how can we resign ourselves to such a fate when
for so many centuries we have claimed to be the educator
of the human race?

The Wild Ass's Skin

By identifying itself with the universal, France has forgotten that it is not alone in the universe, that other societies exist that do not follow its laws, are ignorant of its customs, and hardly know that it exists. We have only to cross the border to see that our prestige is declining, eroded everywhere by Anglo-Saxon dynamism, but also by Indian, Chinese, Brazilian, Arab, and Hispanic dynamism. Because France exists only through the Word, it revels in its grandeur at the same time that the latter is dwindling. The more provincial it becomes, the more it sinks into pathetic vehemence, frenzied lyricism, and empty formulas. The ministry of language, even if flamboyant, is no substitute for action. We have never talked so much about our influence as we have since it began to decline. A small country that thinks it is a great power, France reminds us of those old aristocratic families that have fallen on hard times but eat out of gold vessels and have servants to wait on them at table. But the roof leaks, the walls are crumbling, the dishes are empty, and outside, peasant revolts threaten.

If I had to define the French ailment, I would say that it is characterized by *a unique combination of arrogance and self-hatred*. We combine an unequaled vanity connected with our memories of the glorious seventeenth century and the revolution with a lack of confidence in ourselves that is symptomatic of nations that are falling behind. This is the worst possible case: the French lack both the pride in their country that is so striking in the United States,

India, and China, and without which nothing great can be accomplished (America thinks what it says and says what it thinks, whereas we are a people of sniggerers, eternal adepts of sarcasm), and the curiosity about others, the passion to learn from foreigners, that is a sign of intelligence and reason. With this mentality, we are forced to lose on both levels: pretension prevents us from drawing on others' experience, and doubt paralyzes us. A country that celebrated in 2005, along with the English, its defeat at Trafalgar, and even sent along its best aircraft carrier, but does not dare to commemorate its victory at Austerlitz can only favor a kind of unhealthy glorification of fiasco, a cult of grandiose failure transformed into an imaginary triumph. Whereas America sees in failure a normal modality of change, a step in its self-construction, France sees it as an irrefutable verdict. Every bankruptcy, every dismissal is experienced as an edict of destiny, so firmly anchored is the certainty that one will never find work again and that every mistake is a blade that bars our way to the future. Thus 65 to 75 percent of the young people questioned by several polling organizations aspire to become government employees, so great is the fear of job insecurity.

In this sense, our rebellion against the United States is motivated less by a divergence in points of view than by a similarity in our behavior. (That is why our frenetic anti-Americanism has never prevented us from cooperating on essentials—at the price, it must be said, of a certain schizophrenia). France loves and detests America, and adores detesting it because it resembles it too much and shares with it, on a smaller scale, most of its defects: the same self-conceit, the same claim to be "the indispensable nation" (Jean-Pierre Chevènement and Madeleine Albright), the same moralism mixed with cynicism, but without the power or energy of our cousin across the Atlantic. France retains with respect to America the reflexes of an offended imperialist. The Americans are succeeding where we are failing, and they force us to struggle along behind them, out of breath. We are still repeating their errors when they have already tried a different path. And the more we adopt some of their methods in the domain of work or law, the more we reject this sinister ascendancy. We are for the moment incapable of countering with anything but mockery and remonstrances, incapable of constructing a better model of social justice, economic efficiency, or ethnic cohabitation. What a humiliation for hard-core republicans to see businesses, schools, and television channels quietly adopting certain principles of affirmative action or to see the question of blacks being raised in France under the auspices of Martin Luther King, Jr., and the civil rights movement. Must we admit that in this area as in others, our American cousins are ahead of us? It is true that the New World cannot be a model because there is nothing comparable to it. But it is symptomatic of our state of mind that all our debates are conducted only with reference to the New World (against the capitalism of Wall Street, ethnic groups, segregation, etc.). France looks neither to the South nor to the North nor to the East: it has its gaze fixed on the West, on its transatlantic cousin, the sole object of its resentment and its desire.

An exasperating Lilliputian, berating the whole world, always recognizing its faults too late (consider the dubious episode in Rwanda), France accepts Europe only on the condition that Europe become French. If Europe turns away or chooses other masters, France growls, rages like a pastor scolding his undisciplined flock. However, this rage is accompanied by gullibility: we recall that in the 1960s and 1970s American campuses were invaded by "French Theory," and departments of philosophy, literature, and sociology were inundated, for better or for worse, by deconstructionist discourses castigating "phallogocentrism." For the past fifteen years, the reverse has been happening: in an oscillating movement to which it is accustomed, America is sending back to us doctrines that were born in Europe and that we blindly embrace because they arrive on our shores bearing the stamp "Made in USA." From the end of history to the end of work, by way of the clash of civilizations, France is becoming an unfortunate laboratory for North American chimeras that the elites of these countries are careful not to put into practice in reality. The most ferocious adversaries of the imperial Republic have a remarkable aptitude for copying its defects while at the same time avoiding its good qualities.

Who Are the Reactionaries?

In France, the peculiarity of conservatism is always to express itself in the language of revolution, because the far Left plays the role of the Super-Ego of the Republic, even in the president's office (Jacques Chirac was for a time enthusiastic about the Tobin tax, came up with another tax on airplane tickets, and in 2005 compared the ravages of liberalism with those of communism). It is to the far Left that we have to justify ourselves, and it is the far Left that is preventing the development of a true social democracy on the English Labour Party model or the Scandinavian model: those who act or legislate must measure themselves against this ideological standard that has replaced the Church and moral authorities. All intellectuals bow down before it and embroider nice variations around its fundamental themes: no speech is accepted if it does not begin with a firm condemnation of the market. This political family, which is itself divided, provides the code that everyone has to use and produces the new proletarian chic (even if it no longer has much to do with the working class). Thus we see old 68ers, exhausted courtiers who have repented of all their compromises, all their despicable acts, suddenly going back into action and plunging back into the anticapitalism of their youth: the radicalism of andropause. Everywhere in the middle classes "bourgeois bolshevism" is thriving. There is no artist, no journalist, no actor who does not claim to be subversive, especially if he or she receives a government subsidy. There is no leading figure in the Socialist Party who does not dream of raising a fist and singing the *Internationale* at the end of the party congress. The rebel used to be a man of the people who wanted to shock the bourgeois; now he is a bourgeois who wants to shock the people. All the supporters of immobilism who fight solely to "preserve acquired interests" have to borrow the discourse of the movement, to the point that Leftism has become the senile disease of socialism. This new attachment to the past wrapped in the language of the sans-culottes is rather disconcerting, first because it superposes revolutionary slogans and corporatist demands. Above all, it manifests the same terror with regard to the march of time as it does to the transformations of the world. We now find as many anarchists in the party of order as there are conservatives in the party of progress. (In France, we call reactionaries those intellectuals who continue to take the Enlightenment seriously, remind the Left of its duties, and do not think they have met their obligations by delivering a few diatribes against the icy waters of finance.) Behind an apparent clash, two forms of conservatism, that of the Right and that of the Left, have long since coalesced in France, braking every attempt at wide-ranging reform. That is contemporary France: servile and in revolt, indocile and obsequious, demanding everything from a government that has been turned into a nurse, into a *mater dolorosa* who is expected to dress our wounds, a charitable arbiter supposed to save us from the unknown. The result of the Revolution of 1789 that did away with intermediate bodies and left the individual to confront the state alone is that there is no category of the population that does not depend on the state while at the same time castigating it, there is no lobby that does not demand the state's intercession and is not engaged in an adolescent relationship of rebellion/submission with regard to the powers that be. But it is the same allergy to the status quo that now leads many French in each of the two camps to want a break with the past.

Even the far Left, which is still dreaming of the final revolution and supports any dictatorship provided that it is anticapitalist and anti-American, is no longer anything more than a union of recriminators. See, for example, the unanimous riposte in June 2005 to the proposal made by Jean-Pierre Raffarin, then prime minister, to make Pentecost Monday, which is a holiday, a working day, in order to use the income to improve the condition of the elderly. The proposal may have been maladroit; nonetheless. France immediately rose up like a single person, crying "Don't touch my holiday," an allusion to SOS Racisme's famous slogan, "Don't touch my pal." But here there is no longer any concern about difference, about the oppressed: people just chanted the Balzacian cry of shop-owners clinging to their little privileges. Pettiness is wrapped in the garments of insurrection. That is the new French language: egoism borrows the vocabulary of philanthropy. A miraculous internal conversion of everyone to altruism. The manifest meaning has to be understood as the opposite of the real meaning. When the French call for an uprising, we have to hear in this call praise for the established order and hatred of change. And because the Left, since 1945, has exercised cultural control over the country, it distributes semantic interdictions, imposes its ways of thought, and anyone who wants to express a dissident opinion has to pledge allegiance to its values. Say that you are on the Left, and anything you do is acceptable. Say that you are on the Right, and nothing you do is acceptable. So that only the

Left, strangely, can undertake important reforms, benefit-
ing from a stunned tolerance on the part of the opposite
camp. We have to reflect on an astonishing paradox: France
is entering into global capitalism only from the angle of denying it, through a flood of anathemas that one would be
wrong to take literally. The more it bridles against free enterprise and vituperates against the "yelping, carnivorous
crowd" of owners (Ruskin), the more it liberalizes itself.
Under cover of a hard-core discourse, it is the socialists
who have privatized the economy the most. We need this
linguistic camouflage, these rhetorical veils, in order to accept the unacceptable; frankness horrifies us.

Obsessed by its lost grandeur, France judges itself only
in relation to an idea that it has itself forged, and not to
the reality that surrounds it. It prefers to confront a soli-
tary utopia rather than the states and peoples across its
borders. Contradictorily, it would like to make history
without getting involved in it, enjoy the double status of
a disengaged spectator and a preacher. Thus the political
class has found itself forced to start lying to the French (de
Gaulle in 1958, Mitterand in 1981), that is, to start reassuring them, telling them what they want to hear, even if they
have to change their tune later on: this great people likes
fables and is allergic to the simple, naked truth.

The Triumph of Fear

In most domains, France's only watchwords are "prudence," "preservation," and "precaution." A whole section

of the intelligentsia competes in expressing the rejection of progress, the hatred of modernity, and alarmist predictions. Jeremiad has become the common denominator of the elites. On the contrary, North Americans, who constantly try to colonize a future that is endlessly receding before them, seem to us to have lost all confidence in the powers of time, to be guilty first of all of upsetting established positions. Every innovation—genetically modified organisms, stem cells, nanotechnologies—is received with suspicion, as if it bore the stamp of the devil. The demonstrations against the reform of retirement pensions in 2003 or against the First Employment Contract in 2006 have shown that it is the young, the students, who are henceforth in the van of the party of fear: a whole generation would like to begin life with a job and a pension guaranteed! The French are afraid of the world, afraid of others, and even more afraid of their fear. And they increase their fear by trying to eliminate risk; they are against "running a risk with the hope, if we survive, of obtaining a good" (Condillac). It is a fear without cause and disproportionate to the real threats, but which arises out of a feeling of dispossession, an incapacity to master a universe that is too complex. We show an allergy to adversity that increases our weakness. Fear wins when the most terrifying hypothesis takes precedence over actual events and acquires greater substance than reality. "Fear is mad," Kant said, "it fears even things from which it expects help." There is a spontaneous catastrophism: a possible disaster is immediately seen as inevitable and thus as almost accomplished. We are now scandalized by hot summers and cold winters: the heavens owe us temperate weather or we will prosecute them! We sniggered at the Americans' incompetence in dealing with Hurricane Katrina in September 2005, but when the temperature rose a few degrees in August 2003 it was experienced in France as an Apocalypse, and fifteen thousand elderly people died: "The Battle of the Heat Wave," read a headline in an evening paper in September of the same year, as if the summer heat were the equivalent of Verdun or Stalingrad. Since the windstorm of December 1999, which destroyed part of the French forests, gardens, and city squares, even the most rickety ones, consisting of a bench and a few square meters of grass, are closed at the first snowflake or the first gust of wind. Children can't go there for a snowball fight: the law is strict. Citizens have to be protected whether they want it or not! But to try to eliminate difficulties at any price is to seek the security of the pensioner from the cradle to the grave. What would we do if we, like people in the countries of southern Asia, were subjected to annual monsoons, or, like those in Central America, to typhoons and hurricanes? On the other hand, when government agencies take strong measures to prevent an epidemic, we accuse them of sowing panic, of damaging this or that vocation. The French citizen's demand is self-contradictory: the state owes one both protection and discretion. It has constantly to hold out a helping hand, but that hand has to be invisible and not restrict one's freedom in any way. Take care of me, leave me alone!

Metamorphosis or Decline?

Among Moderns there is a fascination with the theme of decline, a simple inversion of progress that attracts both experts and moralists. It reintroduces the prestige of the ineluctable into humans' free praxis. Anyone who cherishes the idea sees himself as a superior intelligence who has grasped the hidden process of history. Announcing, supported by a raft of statistics, the decline of an empire sets you up as a prophet. For the country or the culture concerned, the news is not necessarily bad: falling is more noble than vegetating; it shows that one had risen very high. The noise one makes when falling has to have repercussions all over the world. There is a certain charm in decay, especially when the cataclysm is slow and mixes distinction with melancholy. Only great families flicker out elegantly, in the splendor of a fading light; ordinary people die ungracefully. Who noticed their existence anyway? Thus France cannot expire like just any nation, it has to theatricalize its fall, tell the whole world about its agony with a grandiloquence that is still a kind of pretension. It invites the whole planet to its funeral. The end has to be majestic and worthy of the past. So many announcements of France's impending death have already been published that we are surprised to find the patient so vigorous. The collapse of a nation rarely resembles the fall of Rome or of communism. Democracies, in particular, have unsuspected resources for survival, for the simple reason that they are plural and defy the predictions of the sociologist, the demographer, or the anthropologist. By definition, our systems display only their defects and conceal their good qualities from the superficial observer's eye: it is easy to single them out for criticism; it is harder to discern the strengths that announce their revival. Nothing allows us to say whether the current crisis is a sign of decay or the first stage in a metamorphosis that we can hardly glimpse. For there is a French miracle: afflicted by a vertiginous debt, structural unemployment, weakened labor unions, a public service that is generous but in crisis, a state that is both obese and impotent, disqualified elites, an educational system that is in complete disarray and suffering from a brain drain and the flight of people with diplomas, France ought to have collapsed long ago. But if cracks are appearing everywhere, it is still hanging on, has carried out many important reforms, has an excellent system for protecting families and a high-level healthcare system, has some of the most dynamic companies in the world, and can even afford to have the highest birthrate in Western Europe. A nation that is living is one that stumbles, and may even go down, but rises up again greater than before. We will not defend French identity by protecting it still more, but rather by bringing it out into the fresh air, preferring boldness to rumination. Identity is not a cage but a point of departure that allows us to add onto the past, to turn it in a different direction. It has always to be reconstructed, and a people, unless it buries itself in its own mausoleum, has to be able to break with its customs, trample on them in order to recharge its batteries. If France does not want to become an object of universal ridicule, it has to expose itself, commit itself still more. Competition from the United States and new, emerging nations is a matter of emulation, not conflict; a challenge, not a defeat. As a symptom of Europe, France could also be the place where Europe is slowly cured of its pathologies, invents itself in a different way. "Where danger is growing, grows also a saving strength" (Hölderlin). In the end, the worst of the conspiracies that threaten us is indifference: not arousing either enough interest or enough anger in others to justify their malice. We have no choice: we have to throw ourselves into the struggle or perish.

Europe without Borders

All or part of Europe's misfortune comes not from the excess but from the absence of borders, especially in its central and eastern parts, where the same regions were successively German, Polish, Russian, Ukrainian, and Austro-Hungarian, peoples were displaced, names changed, and administrations modified. Protecting the small states from the covetousness of the large ones, guaranteeing their borders, was the step that inaugurated modern Europe. A border is not simply a line of demarcation, it is a wound that bleeds, for which people have fought. Some of these wounds heal over, others open up elsewhere. To draw a boundary is to put an end to a battle: the former enemy becomes an ally, the foreigner a neighbor. The border areas calm down, dangers are domesticated. Every boundary carries within itself the utopia of its abolition: many people see in today's Europe a promise open to the whole world, a "civilizational idea" (Edgar Morin) that it would be retrograde to identify with Rome, Athens, or Jerusalem. "We are not unifying states, we are unifying human beings," said Jean Monnet with a very French sense of abstraction.

But Ceuta and Melilla in Morocco, Lampedusa in Italy, the Canaries in Spain, all disembarkation points for African immigrants, remind us that Europe is not the world, not even a second United Nations, and we close our door to the people who are knocking on it. Of course, Europe has always considered its limits as mobile. It has eroded national feeling without for the moment substituting for it a federal or supranational feeling; it has limited the sovereignty of its member states without transferring it to a superior authority. As a result, the body of Europe is fragmented, and its parts come together in a simple collage. It is not Europe that has killed the nations, it is the nations that have exhausted themselves in conflicts that forced them to construct Europe in order to survive. Stripped of the old claim to exclusive possession of the truth, they no longer know who they are, and the extension of the Union accentuates this feeling of paradoxical floating, an uncertainty arising from too much openness. We have moved from national confinement to the fear of the wide-open spaces. Europe is dying from its success: everyone wants to join it at a time when it has doubts about its mission. The old lady still has enough charms to be courted. "The only boundary that the European Union draws is defined by democracy and human rights" (Preamble to the Declaration of Laeken, November 2001). On that principle, India, South Africa, Senegal, Ghana, Canada, Australia, New Zealand, the United States, Japan, South Korea, and a good part of Latin America would be candidates for admission to the European Union. . . . A dream of a cosmopolitan order that would gradually spread over the whole planet.

Timorous and all-devouring, the Old World is in danger of dying, like Rome, of obesity, an ectoplasm that grows larger as it loses its substance. It combines political resignation with the infantile hope of being able to include millions of additional people without difficulties. But the border is not only an obstacle, it is the condition for the exercise of democracy, it establishes a durable link between those sheltered within it and gives them the feeling of belonging to a common world. It separates as much as it unites, it is the door that closes as well as the bridge that connects, it remains open on what it keeps away from us. The true advance in thought as well as in politics is to move the barriers, not to abolish them. One has to have a home in order to open oneself up to the outside, and it is good that nations be separate in order to exist. Europe has to have borders within which it can gather itself together in order to radiate outside its borders. Today, it has to have the courage to say that it is full, and to give up the illusion of unlimitedness: gnawing away at new territories, that imperialism by capillarity, can only be fatal for it. It can encourage regional rearrangements in the Maghreb, in the Near East, and in sub-Saharan Africa, but not assume responsibility for them. Establishing a border is not an act of hostility but a will to establish good relationships. Distance is necessary for communication; too much proximity blurs our view. To ignore geography is to doom oneself to disappear. In other words, there is no history without geography.

CHAPTER EIGHT

Doubt and Faith: The Quarrel between Europe and the United States

Yankees, go home . . . but take me with you!

Every time my thinking becomes too dark

and I despair of Europe, I can find hope

only by thinking of the New World.

—PAUL VALÉRY, 1931

A young millionaire from the American West, Christopher Newman, who has made a large fortune in business, comes to France, curious, like a reverse Christopher Columbus, about the Old World and its customs. As awkward as he is honest, he falls madly in love with a young noblewoman whose hands fascinate him. He courts her with simplicity, tells her naively about all the money that would be at her disposal were she to marry him, and does not dissimulate either his intentions or his character. "I honestly believe I have no hidden vices or nasty tricks. I am kind, kind, kind! Everything that a man can give a woman I will give you."[1] His proposal of marriage is accepted, and he waits patiently, trusting in his fiancé's promise. His candor is fatal to him, and he sees his hopes dashed in a dénouement of a rare wickedness in which his nobility will be severely tested by false and mendacious people.

To Be or to Have

Innocence and sophistication, frankness and duplicity, puerility and old age, good-naturedness and refinement, all these clichés opposing America and Europe have a hard time of it: a cliché is a part of the truth that survives its emergence, even when it has ceased to be true. We might wonder whether at the beginning of the twenty-first century the cardinal opposition between the two halves of the Western world is not instead one between doubt and

[1] Henry James, *The American* (1877; rpt. New York: Rinehart, 1949), p. 117.

faith, disenchantment and hope. A fundamental question:
Why does America, despite its crimes, escape the guilt
that is the rule in Europe, and why does it rise again like a
phoenix from its errors? It has not experienced the "monstrous orgies of hatred" (Paul Claudel) that characterize
the history of Europe; it has experienced neither Verdun
nor Auschwitz; it has not been occupied, devastated, and
degraded for centuries; and despite Hiroshima, it has retained intact the foundations that constitute it. An America
religious to the point of zealotry is often opposed to an
agnostic Europe, which is supposed to live within a purely
immanent horizon. But the faith of America is first of all
a faith *in* America, the certainty that a new Jerusalem is
being built, the certainty of being chosen by Providence to
save the world. On the other side of the Atlantic, religion
is from the outset plural; there are hundreds of denominations, and they accompany the destiny of democracy.
There is nothing comparable to the religious monopoly
that Rome was able to exercise over part of the Old World:
modern Europe has been constructed against the Church,
the United States with the churches. The American God
is eclectic, composed of all the nations that compose that
republic, a benevolent entity that is attentive to the success
and welfare of the faithful.

The Old and the New Worlds incarnate differing con-
ceptions of the Enlightenment: skepticism and the art
of living, on the one hand, and optimism and religious
feeling, on the other. Whereas Europe combines idealism
in international relations with pessimism about change,
America mixes a tragic vision of humanity (the "Axis of

Evil") with the certainty that it is improving. Irenicism, on one hand; realism, on the other. The first position always threatens to turn into immobilism, the second into adventurism. A noble concern to transform the wolf into a lamb, on the one hand; the temptation to reduce the complexity of things to the sole policy of the "Big Stick," on the other. Europe, sated with lies, massacres, and deportations, still dreams of a utopia of happy contagion that would convert its adversaries into partners: if we are nice to them, they will become nice to us. America, on the other hand, is a power capable of designating an enemy, even if it exaggerates the threat. Let's be frank: these fracture lines separate public opinion on the two sides of the Atlantic. When the United States undergoes grave crises, as at the time of the Vietnam War or in Iraq today, it purges itself by means of a collective catharsis, ridiculing its errors, and ridding itself of its evil geniuses. But it does not experience the waves of self-deprecation that in Europe afflict a whole society and affect its mood for a long time. In the United States, guilty conscience is sectorized, limited to certain campuses, to the left wing of the Democratic Party; when the Republicans celebrate the greatness of their country and set out to do battle with their detractors, the latter suggest steps toward social justice (but why would a desire to redistribute wealth be incompatible with greatness, why couldn't there be a patriotic, interventionist Left?). The laughable contortions of political correctness, all the verbal preciousness of ethnic and cultural identity groups that has sterilized research without concretely improving the condition of minorities, has never touched the heart of

national feeling, and especially not the high levels of government. In a word: Europe offers reasons to believe only
in doubt; America offers reasons to doubt only within a
larger faith that includes and absorbs them.

It is the charm and the good fortune of Europe not to
have been completely taken over by capitalism, to have escaped in part from the painful crudeness of money, from
the logic of calculation, from the vulgarity of the reign of
profits, and to still be fraught with bizarre customs, old-
fashioned civilities, and ancient solidarities that form a
fascinating kaleidoscope. To adapt one of Henry James's
formulas, Europe has not erased its reliefs. But the irony
of Europe is that although it is a bastion of socialism and
Marxism, it defines itself only in social and mercantile
terms. Its politicians are primarily traveling salesmen
whom the prospect of juicy contracts renders oddly silent regarding the subject of fundamental rights (as when
they bow down before Putin to get a little gas and oil). The
true spiritual father of the Old World is less Immanuel
Kant or Jean Monnet than Adam Smith, the theoretician
of the *Wealth of Nations*, who held the firm conviction,
revolutionary in his time, that economic prosperity is the
most efficient way of domesticating human passions and
civilizing the world. A pacifying diversion that transforms
barbarians into merchants or, what amounts to the same
thing, protestors against merchandise. (Our alter-globalists and other anti-utilitarians remain under the spell of
a mercantile ethos that obsesses them and from which
they cannot free themselves. Their anticapitalism is the
symptom of their allegiance to the market, on which they

take out all their rebelliousness and energy. They make us think of those atheists who blaspheme against God the better to resuscitate him). How can we help smiling when an American sociologist solemnly informs us that "the new [European] dream is focused not on amassing wealth but, rather, on elevating the human spirit" (Jeremy Rifkin)? Europe is supposed to have become the land of Being, whereas America and Asia are the lands of rapacity and endless accumulation. Let us say instead that Western Europe seems to have lost what the United States has retained: a delicate balance between the desire to get rich and the ideal of freedom, between private interests and collective values. North America combines the most aggressive capitalism and the most insatiable cupidity with spiritual and political counterweights, beginning with patriotism, which we have forgotten. The moral collapse of the Old World, at least in the West, is composed of remorse and comfort, one reinforcing the other, the posture of guilt serving to strengthen the hold of the total consumer. Keeping alive the tension between being and having is what we can no longer do, whereas America, although it has been described as "an air-conditioned nightmare," has remained, voluntarily or involuntarily, a mystical country, a "spiritual principle," as Renan said of the nation. It still moves within the realm of the sacred, whereas we move in the profane universe of purchasing power, standard of living, and petty private happiness (against a background of the chic alibi of high culture). Europe is an unrelenting questioning of its identity, its boundaries, its function; it is at the very heart of an insoluble enigma. Whereas

America asserts itself, Europe questions itself. One says "I want," the other says "Who am I?" Europe has become the receptacle for all the utopias of modernity: it is urged to invent new rules of the game, to contribute, for instance, to the de-Westernization of the world (Raymond Panikkar), to rediscover the poverty that gives rise to cultural life (George Steiner), to encourage the elevation of the human race (Jeremy Rifkin), to establish the reign of the spirit (Gianni Vattimo), to make itself the world's hostage, to put an end to injustice, to bridge the gap between North and South, and so on. But this rhetoric of great designs, this lyricism of the vague, is paid for by the sacrifice of its constitution as a political subject. We choose the impossible, the unimaginable, and the marvelous because we have lost the sense of the possible. The splendid autism of utopia, which closes itself up in its own shell.

The Troublemakers in History

In February 2005 the American secretary of state, Condoleezza Rice, came to Paris to consolidate the improvement in relations between the White House and the Élysée after the crisis over Iraq. Speaking at the Institut d'études politiques, in the heart of the Saint-Germain-des Prés quarter of Paris, she referred to the mission of the democracies, which is to spread freedom and bring down tyrannies: "We know," she said, "that we have deal with the world as it is, but we do not have to accept the world as it is." The French press was astonished and suggested that she had gotten carried away, gone to extremes. This was a strange amnesia, since with these simple words Rice reminded the French, who had forgotten it, of the message of the Revolution of 1789. In this sense, America, although we constantly demonize it, still defends the democratic treasure that we have repressed or relativized. We resent America for having grown as we have dwindled, but especially for having promoted, often in a brutal and cynical way, values to which we pay only lip service because we no longer believe in them. We love it for the wrong reasons (its violence, its excess), but we hate it for its good sides because they remind us of our mission and because it remains the country where democracy is triumphing. In its worst moments, Europe seeks peace at any price, even a bad peace, to use St. Thomas's expression, one that sanctions injustice, arbitrary rule, terror, a detestable peace that is heavy with fatal consequences. Europe postulates freedom for all but is content for it to reign in Europe alone. *Europe has a history but America is history*, it is still driven by an eschatological tendency toward the future. In this sense, it is the last great nation in the West, the only one that is capable of "acting decisively in an exceptional situation" (Carl Schmitt), of rising above its immediate interests to defend its conception of freedom. America generally begins by making mistakes, sometimes criminal ones, but then it corrects them. Europe makes no mistakes because it doesn't try anything. In Europe, prudence is no longer the art defended by the Ancients, that of conducting oneself in an uncertain situation, but rather the ultimate goal of political action. We detest America because it matters. We prefer Europe because it represents neither a threat nor a stake. Repulsion is an indirect homage, friendliness almost a form of scorn.

For the Old World, which thinks it has entered the postnational and posthistorical phase,[2] the major crime committed by the United States, and to a lesser degree by Israel, is to be the troublemakers in history, still stuck in the bloody dramaturgy from which we have extricated ourselves with great effort. "They're still at it!" we exclaim on seeing GIs bogged down in Iraq or Tsahal recruits maneuvering their tanks among Palestinian children. Because of them, the old series of massacres and vengeances threatens to begin again. Their military folly puts us in danger; besides, isn't Islamism an American creation, a Frankenstein that escaped the control of its Yankee godparents? The latter propagate nothing but catastrophe. Old nations, still bearing scars and bruises from their former excesses, admonish the young American superpower and beg it to keep a cool head and renounce war and expansionism. We are the wisdom of the world; America is the madness. As Dominique de Villepin, then France's foreign minister, put it on March 23, 2003, speaking of Iraq:

---

[2] According to Jeremy Rifkin, who hails this development. Whereas patriotic fervor is as strong as ever in America, it is in steady decline in Europe, along with the decline in national pride. Rifkin discerns in American pride a disturbing archaism: "In a globalizing era where allegiance to country is becoming less important in defining individual and collective identity, the fact that Americans remain so passionately committed to the conventional nation-state political model puts us solidly on the side of traditional geopolitics, but hardly in the vanguard of a new global consciousness." Jeremy Rifkin, *The European Dream: How Europe's Vision of the Future Is Quietly Eclipsing the American Dream* (New York: Penguin, 2004), p. 23.

"Europe and France have a head start on other countries. We have survived numerous wars, ordeals, and barbarities, from which we have learned." But Europe can have a beneficial influence on the countries surrounding it only once the area has been pacified and governments have given up settling their disputes by force of arms and are willing to agree to democratic gentleness. Europe, and this is its peculiar genius, absorbs the world by whole nations, whereas America integrates them by communities: Latinos, Chinese, Haitians, Koreans, and so on. In both cases the goal is to neutralize the threat of violence through contracts, constraints, and promises. But for this conversion of a "hostile alterity" (Jean-Louis Bourlanges) to take place, a dissuasive power has to hold in check dictators, hoodlums, and brass hats eager to fight. A credible sheriff is needed, not operetta weapons. It is because NATO represents a serious military threat in Europe that democratic revolutions in Ukraine and Georgia became possible, despite Moscow's hostility to them. Without this strike force, the European Union's virtuous power to propagate democracy by bringing its neighbors into the circle of prosperity and justice would have little chance of succeeding. The perpetual peace to which Europe aspires has its source not in Europe but in the United States.[3]

[3] That is perhaps the type of irritation and fascination that Israel exercises on Europeans. A pioneer state, condemned to death by its neighbors as soon as it was born, seen as an impious tumor in the land of Islam, it serves as a model and a foil for a Europe that has too long abandoned itself to uncertainty and softness. These "Hebrew-speaking Cossacks" (an expression Begin used in speaking of Sharon) who have no remorse but do have consciences and who revive the myth of the founder, remind us that a society is strong only in its beginnings, when it still has the will to fight and to

The Archaism of the Soldier

We no longer like war, and we leave to others the task of waging it, though we criticize them relentlessly when they resort to force of arms. Europe suffers, with respect to its American cousin, from the debtor's complex. It is clearly understood, at least in Western Europe, that without American help in 1917, and especially in 1944, it would have been purely and simply wiped off the map or permanently colonized by Soviet troops. There are generous acts that amount to insults: the Marshall Plan and then the North Atlantic Treaty increased the debt, and America is guilty even for the good deeds it has done us. "I have no enemies," Jules Renard said, "I haven't done favors for anyone." The citizens of the Old World think that by ceasing to kill each other and erecting the slogan "never go to war again" into an untouchable dogma, they have done all that is necessary. This magnificent result, from which many a lesson can be drawn, omits one little detail: Europe, deprived for the moment of credible political and military tools, still depends, as we have seen, on its Yankee big brother for its defense. A strange inconsistency: we never cease cursing the United States but do nothing to free ourselves from its tutelage. The more we vituperate America, the more we make ourselves dependent on it, like a child who revolts against its parents but never leaves them. Why do

---

establish itself. Sure that Europe, in the event of a serious danger, would immediately sacrifice them on the altar of tranquility, the Israelis know that they have to rely on themselves alone. Whether we approve of them or not, we have to recognize in them a constantly lively invitation to resistance.

we consent to be powerless, why have we laid at the feet of our worst ally our capacity to act? Because we consider the soldier an archaic figure, scarcely to be tolerated unless he is made of tin; he has been replaced by the physician, the nurse, the rescuer, the diplomat with modest ambitions and gentler methods. An atavism of democracies required always to prefer their well-being to freedom, to limit themselves to the "little comforts of life" (Tocqueville)? Probably. But if we still believe in violence, if we fear the disorder of our own hoodlums and the infiltration of barbarians from the outside—that is why the policeman, the spy, and the secret agent still enjoy a certain prestige denied the soldier—the rejection of armed conflict is directly connected with the development of individualism and the decline of nationalism. A contemporary person does not want to be dispossessed of his death in a collective flare-up that governments and military staffs cannot control. To die for my country, for an ideology, that is, for a principle superior to my individual existence, has become inconceivable: the old cry of the German pacifists during the Cold War—"Better Red than dead!" (which faintly echoes what Jean Giono said in 1937: "I would rather be a living German than a dead Frenchman"[4])—is now a widely shared conviction in Europe. It would be wrong to describe this attitude as simply cowardice. War leads us to turn away from suffering: we have no control over its development and its consequences. Since, unlike Americans, we have ceased to identify ourselves bodily with a country,

---

[4] Quoted by Richard J. Golsan, *French Writers and the Politics of Complicity* (Baltimore: Johns Hopkins University Press, 2006), p. 83.

we accept only the constraints that we impose on ourselves. Even in the United States, the Bush administration overestimated the determination of its citizens to fight the "Axis of Evil," and forgot the lesson of Vietnam: a liberal people oriented toward prosperity and individual development could not transform itself into a collective soldier and watch its children die in large numbers for a long time without asking whether its enterprises were well-founded. Even when confronted by serious aggression, a hedonist and individualist society obsessed with personal success is naturally reluctant to make sacrifices, regardless of the martial rhetoric used to clothe its ambitions. The United States, which has abolished military conscription and has an army of professional soldiers, can experience moments of great solidarity, long-lasting revivals of patriotism, but it is not suited to run the world because its "message," like that of Europe, is love of life and self-realization. The contemporary individual sets the scene for his own death: if he has to die, he wants to do it with full awareness, not like a rat in the mud of the trenches, in the chaos of battlefields. Our reasons for living exclude any reason for dying for a cause that transcends ourselves or the people we love. We agree to "put our bodies at risk of death" (P. Contamine) only in sports or extreme situations we have chosen. The same people who are prepared to endure inhuman torments while climbing a mountain or crossing a stormy ocean in a small boat, refuse to risk their lives for the survival of a larger whole to which they have only a vague sense of belonging. Modern sacrifice is a game played between the world and myself, from which the collectivity is excluded (or subsists only minimally in the form of the family). To be tolerable, suffering has to be freely chosen, not undergone. Europeans are no more from Venus than Americans are from Mars. But by a strange inconsistency, with the exception of a few countries like France and Britain that still have armies worthy of the name, Europe prefers to leave its overall defense to the United States. It is perhaps wrong, as is shown by the Iranian threat, to suppose that peace can be attained by means of dialogue and good will alone. The only country, Switzerland, whose mountains are full of bomb shelters and whose population is armed, where every citizen has to train regularly for combat, is not even in the European Union and loudly proclaims its neutrality. Europe should at least coordinate its strategic capacities and provide itself with a center of military power capable of making up for American deficiencies, which are becoming increasingly apparent. Persuading our citizens of the necessity of having a strong army that is capable of intervening anywhere would constitute a genuine cultural upheaval.[5]

⁵ In October 2001 France had to rent Russian planes to contribute to the intervention in Afghanistan. Half of its fleet of helicopters was grounded because it had not been properly maintained and lacked replacement parts. Europe, the American journalist Thomas Friedman revealed, has a serious lack of long-range transport aircraft. NATO has only four, all of them British and rented from Boeing, and had to borrow Russian and Ukrainian Antonovs. What would happen if war were to break out at Christmas, when most of these Antonovs, requisitioned by toy companies, are carrying electronic products around the world? Altogether, the armies of the European Union can in theory mobilize two million soldiers in uniform. But only 5 percent of these European troops have the logistic ability to be transported outside Europe to a foreign theater, as opposed to 70 percent of American troops. European troops, some of which are unionized, are suitable for peacekeeping tasks, not for high-intensity combat. Finally, let us recall that in 2005

The Swaggering Colossus

However, inversely, dealing with problems solely from the military angle, to the detriment of political reflection, pounding our chests and swaggering about are not enough. In the past, the United States has paid dearly for its piously simple dream of the messianic nation, its unshakeable conviction that it is the country of the good, the true, and the beautiful, and its naïve belief that everything that is good for Uncle Sam is good for the whole world. The children of an exceptional and elect land, born under divine protection, Americans sometimes seem to want to exempt themselves from the duties incumbent on ordinary humans. The questionable way in which they have recently sought to put themselves above the common law, refusing to ratify certain treaties, laying down rules for others that they don't observe themselves, carrying on a dubious guerrilla war against the International Court of Justice and against the United Nations, whose approval they occasionally seek the better to reject it later, the legal scandal of Guantanamo and Abu Ghraib, the abject use of torture by its army and intelligence services, the arbitrary practice of wiretapping in the name of national security, and finally the hubris of the indispensable nation that needs no counterweight because it balances itself (Madeleine Albright), sometimes remind us of the Marxist

---

American military expenditures amounted to a total of 400 billion dollars, whereas for the same year Europe as a whole spent only half as much. Thomas L. Friedman, "Europe Should Sell Arms to Itself, First," *International Herald Tribune*, March 7, 2005.

regimes that used to reject bourgeois legality in the name of a superior proletarian truth. The danger threatening the United States is not only economic greed but the democratic messianism of which the Bush Doctrine is partly a direct emanation.

The mad dream in the second Gulf War of reshaping the Near East, solely on the basis of a decision made by a team of advisors, has been wrecked by events. The neoconservatives who were the chief architects of this conflict are still Bolsheviks who have moved to the right and who have retained from their old family, Trotskyism, the same Promethean determination to impose their will, the same disregard of facts. There is a certain grandeur, a certain energy, in their view of the world, their cult of creative chaos, their intention to impose democracy by means of bayonets. For the first time, ideology, that European disease, took a durable grip on some of the influential elites in Washington, who tried to force the world to adopt their way of seeing things. But this political engineering collided, as it always does, with the complexity of human affairs. "A neoconservative," Irving Kristol wrote, "is a liberal who has been mugged by reality." We have to conclude that the attack was benign, since it is in fact the reality principle that has suffered most in this area. Democracy cannot emerge full blown from despotism, and it cannot be reduced to a simple electoral process: it is a historical adventure that requires slow maturation, sometimes lasting several centuries, a gradual education in equality and freedom, an acceptance of the peaceful conflict of opinions, and a specific form that breaks with the past but in which the past continues to play an essential role. The democratization of Muslim countries, if it happens, will emerge from Islam, not from its negation.

The Bush administration broke, in a disquieting way, with the combination of empiricism, common sense, and enthusiasm that has always characterized America. Its mistake was not that it was American but that it was not American enough and drew this great country toward an extremism foreign to its traditions. Fortunately, state lies and the absolutism of a faction tempted to violate Constitutional principles were restrained by institutional mechanisms. This forbids us to despair of the American republic: the counterpowers—the system of checks and balances, the media—pull government back toward the center, even if a serious deviation can never be excluded. The culture of mobilizing popular opinion and fear has always been the favorite instrument of dictatorships; democracies can make only a limited use of it without destroying themselves. In such enterprises, there is the danger of adopting the enemy's way of seeing things the better to defeat him, of legislating and militarizing excessively, of setting up a system of generalized surveillance of citizens on the pretext of protecting them, of freezing or weakening the marvelous edifice constructed by the founding fathers; in short, of destroying the parliamentary system in order to save it. The establishment of a new McCarthyism, which attracts certain elements of the most conservative far Right, would constitute Bin Laden's greatest victory over the country of Lincoln. To defend civilization with barbarous weapons is to install barbarity at the very heart of civilization and blur the boundaries between them. "When fighting a monster, beware of becoming a monster yourself" (Nietzsche).

After he had caused Carthage to be razed, the Roman general Scipio imagined, in a dazzling intuition, an identical fate for Rome; he saw the empire killed by his own triumph. The same movement that had raised him to the heights could cast him into the abyss. It is the mark of a great man, the Greek historian Polybius tells us, to realize that victory and ruination can always coincide. The dizziness produced by easy success is a bad counselor if it strengthens a state's or nation's certainty that it is invincible. Contrary to what the neoimperialist lobby that influenced the Bush administration thought, America, far from being invulnerable, does not have the means to be an empire, even a benevolent one. In reality, it is not American leadership that is disquieting, but rather its discretion, the feeling that this occasional policeman, this "part-time sheriff" (R. Haas), is not up to the mission he has assigned himself. An army whose official doctrine is still "zero fatalities" and remains haunted by the debacle in Vietnam is unsuited to long-term military operations, especially when they make no sense to the public. Confronted by a lack of troops, the Pentagon has found itself at the limit of its capacities, engaged as it is in several theaters of operations. Since the end of the Cold War, the illusion of omnipotence has intoxicated certain conservative groups, who confuse being super-powerful with being all-powerful. Unless there is a major crisis, the predominance of the United States cannot continue for more than a decade or two, especially in view of the Asian giants that are emerging. Intoxicated by its strength, America forgot that "the worst enemy of success is success itself" (David Landes), and that it is incapable of assuming alone the burden of a new world order. America is an empire in size, but the American people is not imperialist. It is by nature isolationist, as is shown by the numerous members of Congress who boast of not having a passport because they never travel abroad. Whence the contrast between a country that intends to play a global role and a people that distrusts the outside world. The curt style of the team that came to power with George W. Bush succeeded in annoying even its closest neighbors, Canada and Mexico, and its ukases from another age, its way of treating allies as children sent to stand in the corner if they disobeyed, didn't help. George W. Bush, an unattractive messenger for freedom who combined casualness with boastfulness, succeeded in making his country even more hated by the rest of the world. Unless it bites the dust again, the United States will be forced to emerge from its splendid self-sufficiency. America is more vulnerable than it thinks, and Europe is less weak than it thinks. One should learn moderation, the other pride. It is a historical misfortune that the more fragile should be gnawed by regret, whereas the stronger is carried away by pride. That is why the former theorizes its impotence, while the latter shamelessly displays its superiority. And it is a still great misfortune that they are divided and add to their respective defects the disadvantage of their separation.

Reconciliation

There are at least four means of reconciliation, which may, moreover, be mixed: exhaustion of the combatants, voluntary forgetting, amnesty, and public discussion. In the first case, the combatants lay down their arms without looking into the nature of the massacres; in the second, a pact of silence is made; in the third, the abolition of the past is decreed (if necessary, as in Algeria, with a prohibition of talking about it on pain of being prosecuted for "instrumentalizing the national tragedy"); and in the last case, there is a dialogue between victims and tormentors. This conversation can be subdivided into two strata: either the guilty parties are pointed out for popular punishment, so that the people are reconciled at the expense of its tormentors, or the latter are reintegrated into the national community. The latter is what South Africa accomplished with its Truth and Reconciliation Commission, which will set a legal precedent. By promising the criminals of apartheid immunity in return for the truth, Pretoria defended the principle of a healing rather than a punitive justice. And since "even the worst of racists can improve" (Desmond Tutu), this form of reconciliation seeks to restore the criminal's dignity as a subject, not to hand him over to popular revenge, thus avoiding both the pitfall of a vengeance that produces a countervengeance and that of the public humiliation of a whole part of the national community. The goal is to use mutual gestures to bring victims and tormentors divided by an inexpiable hatred closer together.

The result remains fragile. For "the truth has not been measured, it has been fabricated. To be charitable, we can say that the truth was negotiated. This truth saved South

Africa from the revolutionary abyss. It will be the specter haunting the country's uncertain future."[6] Thus there is a politics of memory that marks out the shape of a possible redemption. In Morocco, this concerns the troubled reign of Hassan II; in Spain, the still open wounds left by Franco's regime; in England, the brutalities of its colonial reign over Ireland; in Cambodia, the horror of the Pol Pot era; in Argentina, the bloody military dictatorship; in Korea, the long, problematic years of the Japanese occupation (1914–1945) and the Cold War; in Russia, the barbarity of communism: the list of countries trying to come to terms with their past grows steadily longer. There are false apologies or apologies so offhand that they are equivalent to a second affront, such as the one offered by the Japanese prime minister, Junichiro Koizumi, apologizing to the Koreans and the Chinese for the atrocities committed by Japanese troops between 1937 and 1945, but nonetheless continuing to honor, in a special sanctuary, Japanese war criminals. Other apologies seem incongruous, as when the Bush administration apologized for the ill-treatment of Americans of Japanese descent during the Second World War, which was good, but said not a word about Native Americans or blacks, whose fate was far more tragic. Even in the young nations of the South, for instance in Africa, the closets are full of skeletons, and bloody stories are constantly emerging, like splinters, from the glorious legend of these new countries. There are no innocent peoples as soon as they are given the opportunity to express themselves politically—that is what

[6] Ebrahim Moosa, quoted by Bogumil Jewsiewicki, "Afrique du Sud: de la vérité de mémoire à la réconciliation," *Le Débat*, no. 122 (November–December 2002), p. 65.

recent history has taught us. Everywhere a great effort to atone for offenses is being made: from the Aborigines of Australia to the Indians of North America, not to mention the Mapuches of Chile, the Inuits of the Great North, or the Pygmies in the Congo, there is no people that is not demanding full investigation into the offenses of which it has been the victim. It is not clear that humanity will be able to deal with this avalanche of demands, engaged as it is in a process of global exorcism of its misdeeds. Crime will always exceed the possibilities of pardon, and memories will always be too numerous: the dead will not be avenged or sufferings amended, wounds closed. Healing is not certain, nor are therapeutic rituals always effective. Too much impossible mourning will remain, too many accursed tragedies. Only history, written or oral, can give these millions of dead the tomb they deserve. One thing is sure: we are only at the beginning of this mechanism. All these expressions of suffering, all these distressing memories are going to multiply because the only inadmissible violence is dissimulation, silence. Humanity has embarked upon a double process of public confession and endless analysis (in which we can see the sign of the universal triumph of Christianity and Freudianism). If there is any lesson that Europe can teach the world, it is the way in which hostile brothers, exhausted by killings, have been reconciled at the edge of the abyss, putting an end to intractable quarrels, and proving that the bitterest heritages can be overcome.

A Poisoned Gift

Europe will be killed by this principle:

"It doesn't concern me."

—GUSTAV MAHLER

Inspired by St. Bernard, the Jesuit Louis Bourdaloue, a famous preacher at the court of Louis XIV, distinguished four kinds of consciences: the good and peaceful (Paradise), the good and troubled (Purgatory), the bad and troubled (Hell), and the bad and peaceful (despair).[1] How can we fail to see that contemporary Europe falls into the last category? We have rarely seen all a continent's elites embrace culpability with such enthusiasm, to the point of taking responsibility for others' faults, volunteering for the most distant catastrophes, and crying "I'm remorseful, I'm remorseful, who has a crime?" Culpability suits us: it provides an alibi for our abdication. It reflects the ultimately rather comfortable coexistence of fear and calm, disavowal and good digestion. We clothe ourselves in the cast-off garb of the perpetual criminal the better to keep ourselves at a distance. There is something frivolous about our itch to be castigated, in our consent to servitude. The trial of Europe continues, enthusiastically conducted by Europe itself. Proud of its ostentatious mea culpa, it claims a universal and apostolic monopoly on barbarity. Its true desire is not conquest but divorce from the world, shelter against the storm. It would like to seal itself up in the cocoon of repentance, abandon itself solely to the sad paradise of the supermarket, a high standard of living, and hedonism.

Thus we have to change the way we see ourselves, undertake a complete reversal of values. In the first place, we have to re-establish our transatlantic ties. The United

---

[1] Quoted in Jankélévitch, "La mauvaise conscience," p. 147.

States can no more do without us than we can do without the United States. America has the exuberance and energy that we need so much. Despite mutual suspicions, we are destined to have a closer relationship, to share the same burdens. Democracies have to be powerfully armed in order not to be defeated by the forces of tyranny. They are the depositories of an infinitely perishable and fragile treasure: human rights, respect for principles. They are responsible for the perpetuation of democracy itself. Europe, if it wants to have any influence at all, must build, alongside its great neighbor, a second entity, unprecedented in its ambitions and its political form, arising from peoples' voluntary agreement to give up part of their national sovereignty. In response to supporters of the great schism that demands a divorce and sees the Atlantic Ocean as a metaphysical barrier separating two incompatible philosophies, we must say that this rivalry has to be converted into an emulation between two blocs that have much to learn from each other in terms of audacity and prudence: tempering American enthusiasm with European level-headedness and European reason with American dynamism. It is not a question of choosing between the Old and the New Worlds, but of a dialectical encounter between the two that is stimulating and generates fruitful contrasts. We have to bring together the two confused halves of the West because, with the notable exceptions of India and Japan, they are the only guarantees of pluralist political systems. And what do we care about semantic quarrels over the meaning of "the West," whether it there is one West or several, whether we should abandon the term or not, provided that the West remains a subversive principle that challenges traditions and arbitrary power, promotes freedom, and forbids each nation to turn inward on itself (that is why "Western values" are so now execrated by all kinds of fanaticism, from Muslim fundamentalism to radical Polish nationalism). Reconciling Europe with history and the United States with the world—that is our task at the beginning of the twenty-first century. Teaching the former that battles are not won by compromise and incantation alone; and teaching the latter that it is not the only country on Earth, invested with a providential mission that makes it unnecessary for it to seek the approval of others, to listen and to debate, that trying to do what is good for people no matter what they want is a recipe for disaster. That we do not have the right to be stupid in the fight against terrorism, at the risk of feeding the flames we are trying to put out. If America were to collapse tomorrow, Europe would fall like a house of cards; it would return to the tergiversation it showed in Munich in 1938 and be reduced to a deluxe sanatorium ready to allow itself to be torn apart, piece by piece, by all sorts of predators. But if Europe were to be dismembered in this way, America's prospects would not be bright, either; it would stiffen into a touchy nationalism, an Orwellian isolationism. On the other hand, every time Europe and America cooperate on a specific project, they achieve marvelous results.

To what must we remain loyal? To the black pages in our history or to the way in which we have learned from them? To the long litany of massacres or to the effort made to emerge from servitude and inequity? In the confrontation of the diverse heritages that constitute us, it is better to praise the triumphs than the mourning, for triumph is mourning plus its transcendence; it is suffering endured and overcome, a collective effort to defy misfortune. Our selective hypermnesia recalls only the calamities, never the highpoints. Why should we take responsibility for the dark periods alone and erase the light that followed them? We can always construct another genealogy; let us seek out ancestors who are honorable rather than wretched. We need to celebrate heroes instead of scoundrels, righteous persons, not traitors, and remain loyal to what is best in us. To the duty to remember we need to oppose the duty to our glories. Confronted by distress, we need to recall the perils we have overcome, to remain firm when everything around us is falling apart, when acts of cowardice and treachery are legion: "Be steadfast, my heart, you have already endured crueler ordeals" (Ulysses). A continent that has come to the edge of the abyss so many times and has drawn back, that emerged from the apocalypse of the Second World War, does not need to feel ashamed of itself. We have to invert our relationship to the past, seeing in it not a source of lament but of confidence. Europe cannot be so desired by others and so unloved by itself when it is the paradigm of barbarity successfully overcome, of a harmonious marriage of power and conscience.

There is no solution for Europe other than deepening the democratic values it invented. It does not need a geographical extension, absurdly drawn out to the ends of the Earth; what it needs is an intensification of its soul, a condensation of its strengths. It is one of the rare places on this planet where something absolutely unprecedented is happening, without its people even knowing it, so much do they take miracles for granted. Beyond imprecation and apology, we have to express our delighted amazement that we live on this continent and not another. Europe, the planet's moral compass, has sobered up after the intoxication of conquest and has acquired a sense of the fragility of human affairs. It has to rediscover its civilizing capabilities, not recover its taste for blood and carnage, chiefly for spiritual advances. But the spirit of penitence must not smother the spirit of resistance. Europe must cherish freedom as its most precious possession and teach it to schoolchildren. It must also celebrate the beauty of discord and divest itself of its sick allergy to confrontation, not be afraid to point out the enemy, and combine firmness with regard to governments and generosity with regard to peoples. In short, it must simply reconnect with the subversive richness of its ideas and the vitality of its founding principles.

Naturally, we will continue to speak the double language of fidelity and rupture, to oscillate between being a prosecutor and a defense lawyer. That is our mental hygiene: we are forced to be both the knife and the wound, the blade that cuts and the hand that heals. The first duty of a democracy is not to ruminate on old evils, it is to relentlessly denounce its present crimes and failures. This requires reciprocity, with everyone applying the same rule. We must have done with the blackmail of culpability, cease to sacrifice ourselves to our persecutors. A policy of friendship cannot be founded on the false principle: we take the opprobrium, you take the forgiveness. Once we have recognized any faults we may have, then the prosecution must turn against the accusers and subject them to constant criticism as well. Let us cease to confuse the necessary evaluation of ourselves with moralizing masochism. There comes a time when remorse becomes a second offense that adds to the first without canceling it. Let us inject in others a poison that has long gnawed away at us: shame. A little guilty conscience in Teheran, Riyadh, Karachi, Moscow, Beijing, Havana, Caracas, Algiers, Damascus, Rangoon, Harare, and Khartoum, to mention them alone, would do these governments, and especially their people, a lot of good. The finest gift Europe could give the world would be to offer it the spirit of critical examination that it has conceived and that has saved it from so many perils. It is a poisoned gift, but one that is indispensable for the survival of humanity.

The first decade of the twenty-first century seems to have been characterized by a decline in Western influence, which may be temporary: the crisis of the economic models proposed by the Thatcher and Reagan governments and their well-known consequences; the impossibility of winning a military victory in Afghanistan and Pakistan; the rise of the Chinese model, which combines political authoritarianism with hypercapitalism; and the booming irruption of great emerging countries onto the international scene. Anglo-American hegemony over the planet has run its course, even if no other has yet replaced it. This is the Obama moment, both a tremendous outburst on the part of the American people and the end of post–Cold War triumphalism, a belated recognition of the limits of superpower. Our civilizations thought they were global, and they were merely provincial. The long Western domination that began with the Renaissance in Europe and was prolonged in the New World is coming to a close: a history is now beginning in which we will no longer be the sole actors and that escapes our control. The earlier vanquished peoples, the ex-colonized, are conquering their former masters and aspire to play by new rules. This is not necessarily a bad thing.

After 1989 Western democracies yielded to the temptation to try to convert everyone in the name of human rights. They postulated that their values were globally valid, despite the fact that many countries, and not the least important ones, continued to reject them (China, Russia, Iran, and others). To the West's excessive indifference, visible in Bosnia and Rwanda, corresponded an excess of interference in Somalia in 1993 and in Iraq in 2003, when we claimed to be saving people from famine or dictatorship in spite of themselves. (Even though the situation in Baghdad has been slowly improving after seven years of chaos, and though Iraqis now enjoy more democracy than they did under Saddam, the human cost is so high that it has turned out to be dissuasive. It remains that the numerous pacifists who took to the streets in Europe and in the United States during the winter of 2003 were unwittingly supporting one of the worst dictatorships in the Middle East. Iraq was an exemplary case of the double bind: whether one approved of the intervention or not, one was wrong.) It is therefore essential that the new Obama administration, with its ability to overcome contraries, substituted a strategy of cooperation for a strategy of confrontation and understood that the war against terrorism had blinded our political elites, increased the number of pluralism's enemies, and strengthened extremists. Seeking to deliver democracy by forceps everywhere on the planet and to impose it by force of arms merely rubbed people the wrong way and threw them into the arms of dictators.

But the politics of the outstretched hand works only when it is reciprocal; its refusal by numerous despotic governments proves that in this area good will is not enough. It would be too bad if the United States, after having moved closer to Europe in the domain of foreign policy (multilateralism, for instance), also contracted its timidity and its tendency to adopt a wait-and-see attitude.

People who hope to see local versions of the Parliament in Westminster established in Kabul, Riyadh, Algiers, and Moscow will have to be patient and learn to accept necessity. The fact that many nations still live under the yoke of arbitrary power and violence may sadden us, but we should not therefore conclude that our own ideals are not valid. After all, those ideals took centuries to take root in our societies. Freedom is not a crusade, it is a proposition. If hundreds of millions of people decline the invitation, that is because they do not find it suitable, and it will be necessary to reformulate it in a different way. Persuasion by example is better than indoctrination by force.

What, for example, should we say about the great imperial groups constituted by Russia and China, which are neither friends nor enemies, and which will still retain an intermediary status? Their size forbids us to mount a frontal attack on them; their police practices forbid us to treat them indulgently. They are simultaneously partners and threats. As partners, we have to trade with them on clear bases, and ask for their help in dealing with the thorny question of Iran and more generally that of global warming. Since they are tyrannical regimes, we have to combine concession and retaliation, firmness and compromise, and develop a strategy that is both flexible and consistent: tell these governments the truth, call a crime a crime, help democrats and dissidents in civil society everywhere. Between confrontation and peace, there is a gray zone that is called political intelligence and that rejects both swaggering and renunciations. Let us avoid a double error: that of seeing other countries in our own image and believing them to be doomed to barbarity and obscurantism. The events in Iran during the summer of 2009 refute these two illusions. We have to recognize both the unity of humankind and the nonconcordance of the different parts of humanity. That presupposes avoiding aggressive proselytizing as well as the spirit of surrender disguised as a dialogue between cultures.

The only war that ultimately matters, as we have known since the Enlightenment, is the war of ideas that is waged day and night, attacking iniquities and denouncing scandals. It is this war, and not torture or bombing, that changes mentalities in depth, improves the condition of women and children, and leads religious believers to live their faith in a more tolerant way and to revise the most aggressive postulates of their sacred scriptures. This war has one defect: it is long. It extends beyond the term of a legislature, goes on over generations and even centuries. To win it, through education, the media, and culture, we have to use the weapons of reason and eloquence. We have to combine our impatience for freedom with the wisdom to wait.

✢ The current book pursues further a line of thought begun in my book *Le Sanglot de l'homme blanc* (Paris: Seuil, 1983); translated by William R. Beer as *The Tears of the White Man: Compassion as Contempt* (New York: Free Press, 1986). In particular, it develops the argument of an article published in May 2003 in the *Revue des deux mondes* entitled "L'Europe et l'Amérique, la fatigue et l'enthousmiasme," reprinted in *Dissent* and *South Central Review* (USA) as well as in *Letra libres* (Mexico).

✢ Publisher's note: The original French version of this book contained quotations from English-language sources that were translated into French. Where possible, the original English wording has been used here. In some cases, where the original sources could not be found, we have translated from French back into English.

Abel, Olivier, 40
Africa/Africans: accountability
  for actions in, 99–100; independent post-colonial, disaster
  of, 11–12. *See also* names of
  countries
Agamben, Giorgio, 22
Ahmadinejad, Mahmoud, 84
Albright, Madeleine, 178, 207
Algeria: apology from France,
  demand for, 43n.10; cry for vi-
  sas to enter France, 12; French
  admission of dissemblance
  regarding, 41n; the French
  colonial experience in, 74–75;
  French control of, obstinacy
  of supporters of, 31–32; Front
  de libération nationale, 30;
  Hitlerizing the colonial history
  of, 119–25
Algerian National Movement, 124
Alidières, Bernard, 124n
Al-Qaeda, 84
Amara, Fadela, 47
Amélie Poulain, 93
Annan, Kofi, 11

anthropocentrism of Western
  self-hatred, 35–36
anti-Occidentalism, 9–11. *See also*
  Third Worldism
Appel des Indigènes, 130
Aquinas, St. Thomas, 200
Arafat, Yasser, 60, 61n.1
Aragon, Louis, 9–10
Arendt, Hannah, 122, 137, 166
Aristotle, 155
Arkoun, Mohammed, 47
Armed Islamic Group, 124
Aron, Raymond, 32, 107, 170
Arouet, Françoise-Marie (Vol-
  taire), 50, 53
Ates, Seyran, 47, 151n
Auschwitz. *See* Shoah, the
Aziz, Tariq, 45n
Aznar, José, 15

Badiou, Alain, 77n.23
Bairoch, Paul, 133–34
barbarity, uses of, 72–73
Barnavi, Élie, 69
Baudrillard, Jean, 14–15, 77
Beck, Ulrich, 92

Benigni, Roberto, 93
Ben Jalloun, Tahar, 58
Ben Mansour, Latifa, 47
Benoist, Alain, 82
Benslam, Fetih, 47
Bensoussan, Georges, 32, 123
Berman, Paul, 19
Bernard, Philippe, 129n.23
Besancenot, Olivier, 175
Beyle, Marie-Henri (Stendhal), 95, 170
Bleich, Erik, 135n
Blondy, Alpha, 132n.26
Bodichon, Eugène, 119
Boniface, Pascal, 18, 78–79n.25
borders, 189–91
Bosnia, 97
Bouchared, Rachid, 141
Bourdaloue, Louis, 216
Bourlanges, Jean-Louis, 202
Bouteflika, Abdelaziz, 123–24
Bové, José, 78
Brandt, Willy, 41
Breytenbach, Breyten, 77n.22
Britain. See Great Britain
Bugeaud, Thomas Robert, 121
Burgat, François, 17
Bush, George W., 32–33, 64n, 65n, 81–82, 211
Bush Doctrine, 208

Canada, special legal provisions for Muslims, 151
Carlos. See Sánchez, Ilich Ramirez
Catholic Church. See Roman Catholic Church

Catholic Committee against Hunger and for Development, 135
Cervello, Mariella Villasante, 22
Césaire, Aimé, 85, 117–18
Chávez, Hugo, 13
Chebel, Malek, 47
Chevènement, Jean-Pierre, 178
China, 225–26
Chirac, Jacques, 12, 41, 97n, 128, 133, 141n, 180
Christianity: anticlerical struggles, violence of past, 48–49; the Palestinians and, 61; secularism, admission of the principle of, 43; Western self-hatred and, 34–35n. See also Roman Catholic Church
Christo, 96
Cioran, Emil M., 34n
Civil Rights Act of 1964, 90
Claudel, Paul, 195
Clinton, Bill, 41n, 82
Cohen, Daniel, 134n
colonialism: colonization and, distinction between, 30–32; as common to all great civilizations, 31n; death of from a double contradiction, 29–30, 33; de facto segregation, inevitability of, 39; as forerunner of Nazism, 119–25; French, reasons for, 74–75; missionaries and the government, relationship of, 29n; oppression under, Hitler's contribution to, 115; trial of and nostalgia for, 127–36. See also decolonization

Conan, Eric, 46n
Condillac, Étienne Bonnot de, 184
consciences, kinds of, 216
Contamine, P., 205
culpability, European embrace
    of, 216
cultural relativism, Islamophobia
    and, 48
"Curse of Ham," 85

Daniel, Jean, 76
Dead White European Males
    (DWEMs), 92
decolonization: hatred of the
    West and, 36–39; legacy of, 11–
    13; low-cost housing projects
    and the narrative of, 164; re-
    sponsibility of former colonial
    powers after, 99–100; Western
    anthropocentrism and, 35–36.
    See also colonialism
de Gaulle, Charles, 133, 168, 183
Dejours, Christophe, 122n
de Klerk, Frederik Willem, 109
Deleuze, Gilles, 68
democracy: barbarity and, 72–73;
    European *vs.* American ver-
    sions of, 88–90; Europe's need
    to reconnect to, 219–20; fear of,
    hatred of the West and, 36–38;
    promoting by force, failure
    of, 224–25; requirements for,
    208–9
Denmark: abolition of slavery in,
    155; caricatures of Muhammad
    in, 5n.19, 54–55, 63–64, 97–98
Derrida, Jacques, 19–22

Diderot, Denis, 73
Doctor Faustus (Mann), 102–3
Dostoyevsky, Fyodor, 5, 83
Dreyfus, Alfred, 78
Durban Conference, 67
duty of memory, the, 157–63

Ellison, Ralph, 140
Éluard, Paul, 137
enemies, utility of, 137–38
Engels, Friedrich, 166
entrism, 25
Esclangon-Morin, Valérie,
    129n.23
Europe: comparisons and con-
    trasts between America and
    (*see* Old and New Worlds). *See
    also* names of countries
European Union: caricatures of
    Muhammad, actions regard-
    ing, 97–98; expansionism of,
    190; NATO's power, depen-
    dence on, 202; Turkish entry
    into, concerns regarding, 37n
Euskadi Ta Askatasuna (ETA), 15

Fanon, Frantz, 116, 161
Faulkner, William, 143
Ferro, Marc, 31n, 100, 172n.2
Ferry, Jean-Marc, 7
Ferry, Jules, 31, 74
Ferry, Luc, 108
Fillon, François, 143n
Fisk, Robert, 45n
Flaubert, Gustave, 109
Foucault, Michel, 69
Françafrique, 133

France: abolition of slavery, 155;
the ailment of, 176–79; Algeria
and (see Algeria); colonialism: trial of and nostalgia for,
127–36; colonialism and collaboration as past sins of, 74–75;
decline or metamorphosis of?,
186–88; declining status of,
struggling to cope with, 168–76;
deportation of Jews, shame of,
75; Greco-Roman culture, impact of, 31; guilt not part of the
self-perceived history of, 7; illnesses of Europe, embodiment
of, 168; Jews, attacks on and
abandonment of in favor of the
Palestinians, 77–80; minorities
in, abstraction of the Citizen
and, 140; national repentance,
deferred truth and the struggle
with, 41–42; paradoxes of,
abominations and principles
of the Republic as example
of, 29; political ideology in,
179–83; rebellious consumers in
the low-cost housing projects,
164–66; Shoah, discussion of
and the treatment of returning
Jews, 112; the triumph of fear
in, 183–85; victims, creation of
governmental entities to support, 152–53
Freud, Sigmund, 72, 104–5
Friedman, Thomas, 206n

Gaarder, Jostein, 70
Gaia (goddess), 35

Gauthier, Florence, 30
Geisser, Vincent, 51n.18
Genet, Jean, 58
Genocide Day, proposal for, 116n
genocide(s): conceptualization
of, 32; perceptions of post-
Nuremberg, 115–17; the Shoah
(see Shoah, the)
Germany: proposal of minor-
ity status for Muslims, 151n;
reconstruction of the Frauen-
kirche in Dresden, 93; the sins
and resurrection of, 102–4
Ghana, 146n
Giblin, Béatrice, 132n.27
Giono, Jean, 204
Girardet, Raoul, 74–75
Giscard d'Estaing, Valery, 133
Glucksmann, André, 113
Goebbels, Joseph, 68
Grandmaison, Olivier Le Cour,
119–22
Grass, Günter, 111
Great Britain: abolition of slavery
in, 155; London, July 7 terrorist
attacks in, 16; opinions of Mus-
lims living in, 145n; sources
of terrorism in, Le Carré's
explanation of, 16–17
Guevara, Ernesto "Che," 61

Haas, R., 210
Habermas, Jürgen, 83n.29
Halimi, Ilan, 77
Hassan II (king of Morocco), 62
Hegel, Georg Wilhelm Friedrich,
97, 101, 105, 167

Heidegger, Martin, 83
Hergé, 1
Herodotus, 105
Hirsi Ali, Ayaan, 47
history: cleansing of and
  pacification, 93–96; Europe's
  relationship to the past, need
  for an inversion of, 218–19;
  Hitlerizing, 117–27; memory
  of old persecutions, question
  of, 157–63; misinterpretations
  of Auschwitz, 113–17; twofold
  lesson of, 106–7; the victim's
  claims on, 140–48 (see also
  victims and victimization)
Hitler, Adolf: recasting history
  in terms of, 117–27; "would
  have made a good Muslim,"
  79n.26
Hobsbawm, Eric, 111
Hölderlin, Friedrich, 188
Holmes, Larry, 139
Holocaust, the. See Shoah
human rights: democracies as
  the repository of, 217 (see also
  democracy); hatred of the
  West and resistance to embrac-
  ing, 36–38
Huntington, Samuel, 83
Hussein, Saddam, 11, 116n, 171n

"ideologization of tradition," 25
India, 136
Innocent III, 43
Intifada(s), the, 59–60, 69
Invisible Man, The (Ellison), 140
Iran, 225–26

Iraq: double bind, intervention
  in as a case of the, 224; French
  public support for Saddam in
  the 2003 war in, 171n; ideological fantasy driving Bush
  administration actions in,
  208–9; invasion of, opposition
  of Catholic Church to, 45n;
  protesters against the 2003 war
  in, 99; Spanish withdrawal of
  troops from, 15
Isabella (queen of Spain), 43
Islam: caricatures of Muhammad
  in Denmark, 51n.19, 54–55,
  63–64, 97–98; criticism of,
  need for, 46–47; criticism of
  equated with Nazi racism, 116;
  Europe, attempt to take over,
  32; fundamentalists vs. reformers in, 52; fundamentalist
  terrorists as an enemy, impact
  of, 137–38; the Palestinians and
  (see Palestinians, the)
Islamic Salvation Front, 124
Islamo-Fascism, 54–55
Islamo-Leftism, 25–26
Islamophobia, 47–53
Israel: blunders of, disproportionate focus on, 64–65;
  casting as force of Oppression
  against the Palestinians, 59–60
  (see also Palestinians); as
  chief menace to world peace,
  perception of, 65; condemnation of, 63–67, 75–76;
  German reparations payments,
  debate regarding, 162n;

Israel: *(continued)*
moral exemplar, squandering
of image as, 69; as reincarnation of the Third Reich, 67–71;
shifting the blame to, 58, 80; as
a troublemaker in history, 201,
202–3n. *See also* Jews and
Judaism; Zionism

James, Henry, 194, 197
Jankélévitch, Vladimir, 67–68n.9,
81
Jaspers, Karl, 115
Jews and Judaism: attacks on and
abandonment of in France,
77–80; condemnation of Israel
and, Europe's past offenses
and, 62–67, 75–80; Israel and
Zionism, relationship with,
66–67, 71; Jewish communities
in Europe, size of national,
102; as problematic elect,
112–13; slave trade, prohibition
from participating in, 156–57;
solidarity of the excluded
shattered by competition over
victimhood, 116–17; Zionism
and Nazism, parallel drawn
between, 67–71. *See also* Israel;
Shoah, the
John Paul II, 44, 113
Johnson, Lyndon, 90
Jospin, Lionel, 78n.25
Jünger, Ernst, 120

Kant, Immanuel, 89, 184, 197
Kelek, Necla, 151n

Kertész, Imre, 112
Khosrokhavar, Farhad, 17
King, Martin Luther, Jr., 178
Kobayashi, Yoshinori, 104
Koizumi, Junichiro, 213
Kosovo, 97
Krim, Abd el-, 9
Kristol, Irving, 208

Lacoste, Robert, 31
Landes, David, 211
Lapeyronnie, Didier, 131n
La Rochefoucauld, François de,
35n, 87
Latouche, Serge, 8, 10, 23–24
Le Carré, John, 16–17
Lemaire, Sandrine, 142n
Lemkin, Raphaël, 119
Leopold II (king of Belgium), 123
Leo XIII, 44n
Le Parisien, 16
Lessing, Gotthold Ephraim, 45
Levi, Primo, 157
Levinas, Emmanuel, 69, 78
Lévi-Strauss, Claude, 7
Lewis, Bernard, 70
Liauzu, Claude, 159
liberalism, French rejection of,
170
Liberazione, 71n.14
Lichtenberg, [Georg Christoph?],
100
Life is Beautiful (Benigni), 93
Limbach, Jutta, 151n
Lindqvist, Sven, 9
litigation. *See* trials and litigation
Livingstone, Ken, 16

Louis XIV (king of France), 123
Lucretius, Titus, 107
"Lunatic," 153
Luther, Martin, 40

Mahler, Gustav, 215
Mandela, Nelson, 109
Manji, Irshad, 47
Mann, Thomas, 83, 102–3
Marco, Enric, 114n.2
Marcos, Subcommander, 58
masochism of Europe, 91–93
Mauritania, 155
Mbembe, Achille, 133
Meddeb, Abdelwahab, 47
memory, 157–62
Merleau-Ponty, Maurice, 13–14
Messali Hadj, Ahmed, 124
Meynier, Gilbert, 123n
Mildenstein, Leopold Itz von, 68
Millet, Kate, 48
Milner, Jean-Claude, 67n.8
Milošević, Slobodan, 82
Ministère Amer, 153
minorities: the politics of identity
    and, 148–52; victimization, dan-
    gers of the appeal to, 140–48
Mitterand, François, 31, 133, 183
Mollet, Guy, 31
Monnet, Jean, 189, 197
Monsieur R, 153
Montaron, Georges, 61
Montesquieu, Charles-Louis de
    Secondat, Baron de, 38, 170–71
Moore, Michael, 82
Moosa, Ebrahim, 213n
Morgenthau plan, 103

Morin, Edgar, 7–8, 62, 70, 189
Morocco, 97, 125
Muhammad, caricatures of,
    51n.19, 54–55, 63–64, 97–98
multiculturalism: ambiguity of,
    the politics of identity and,
    148–52; "prides" (gay, black,
    etc.), problem of, 145–46. See
    also minorities
mutilation, "short-sleeve" and
    "long-sleeve," 12

Naïr, Sami, 70
Napoleon Bonaparte, 118–19
Nasreen, Taslima, 47
NATO. See North Atlantic Treaty
    Organization
Near East: Israel (see Israel);
    Israel and Judaism, functions
    served by vilifying, 62–67;
    Jews/Zionists and Nazis,
    parallel drawn between in the
    context of, 67–71; Western in-
    fatuation with events in, 59–62
neoconservatives, 208
Nietzsche, Friedrich, 2, 137, 210
Nora, Pierre, 158
North Atlantic Treaty Organiza-
    tion (NATO), 202

Obama, Barack, 149
Obin report, 143n
Old and New Worlds: compared
    and contrasted, 91–93, 96,
    194–99; decoupling as strategy
    of Europe, Al-Qaeda, and
    Ahmadinejad, 82–84;

Old and New Worlds: *(continued)*
democracy, differing ver-
sions of, 88–90; European
anti-Americanism, 80–84;
the French perspective on
America, 170–71, 176–78; international relations, approaches
to, 199–202; lessons to be
learned by, 211; military power,
203–6; ties between, need
for a dialectical encounter to
strengthen, 216–18
Orban, Viktor, 94
Organization of the Islamic Conference, 49–50
Ottoman Empire, 31, 155
Oz, Amos, 61

pacification, 94–95
Palestinians, the: abandonment
of the Jews in France by sup-
porters of, 77–80; as mythi-
cal idea/icon for Europeans,
58–59; Western elites' tolerance
for terrorism by, 76–77; West-
ern infatuation with, 59–62
Panikkar, Raymond, 199
Péguy, Charles, 67, 171
Perejil, 97
Pinter, Harold, 81–82
Pius VII, 44n
Plumelle-Uribe, Rosa Amelia, 23,
117, 126n
Pol Pot, 11
Polybius, 210
Powell, Colin, 97, 149

Prodi, Romano, 71n.14
Putin, Vladimir, 36

race and racism: in the Arab
Muslim world, 156; converting a stigmata into a privilege
and the revival of, 85–86;
overcoming memory to end,
163; victimization and, 140–48;
white skin as a moral defect,
the evil of the West and, 23
Racine, Jean-Luc, 136n
Radjub, Jibril, 61n.1
Raffarin, Jean-Pierre, 182
Rahman, M. Abdul, 50n
Ramadan, Tariq, 116
Raybaud, Antoine, 173n
reconciliation, 212–14
Renan, Ernest, 162, 198
Renard, Jean, 203
repentance: admission and
apologies, condescendence
embedded in Western politics
of, 40–43; Christianity and, 45;
eluding responsibility through,
96–100; enlargement of the
circle of, need for, 42–43; the
penitence-state and, 108–9;
remorse and, distinction
between, 40
Ribbe, Claude, 118–19
Rice, Condoleezza, 149, 199–200
Rifkin, Jeremy, 198–99, 201n
Robitaille, Antoine, 24n.24
rogue states, 21–22
Rollot, Catherine, 129n.23

Roman Catholic Church: betrayal and support for the spirit of the Gospels by, 43–45; Iraq, opposition to invasion of, 45n
Roosevelt, Franklin Delano, 103
Rosanvallon, Pierre, 88–89n
Rousso, Henry, 157n
Roy, Oliver, 51n.19
Rushdie, Salman, 48
Ruskin, John, 183
Russia, 225–26

Sacranie, Sir Iqbal, 116n
Saint-Arnaud, Jacques Leroy de, 121
Sala-Molins, Louis, 23, 160–61
Sallenave, Danièle, 70
Sánchez, Ilich Ramirez (a.k.a. "Carlos"), 25
Sankho, Foday, 12
Saramago, José, 71n.15, 77n.22
Sartre, Jean-Paul, 90
Saudi Arabia, 155
Schmitt, Carl, 167, 200
Scipio Africanus, Publius Cornelius, 210
selective immigration, 132n.26
self-denigration as self-glorification, 34–36
self-esteem, recovery of, 100–106
Sen, Amartya, 107
Senghor, Léopold Sédar, 27
Sepúlveda, Luis, 71n.15
Shariati, Ali, 25
Sharon, Ariel, 60, 65n, 69
Shayegan, Daryus, 25

Shoah, the: Auschwitz as the West's civil religion, 112; blaming Israel to avoid taking responsibility for, 80; commemoration leading to rejection and dismissal of, 112–13; the duty of memory regarding, 157–58; Hitlerizing history based on, 117–27; misinterpretations of, 113–17; victimhood and (see victims and victimization)
Shooting Star, The (Hergé), 1
Singh, Manmohan, 136
slavery: abolition of, selective memory of the history of, 155–57; contemporary continuation of, 157; Nazification of, 125–26; reparations for, demanding, 159–61; the Roman Catholic Church's position on, 43–44
Sleeper, Jim, 85
Smith, Adam, 197
Soares, Mario, 19
Socialist Workers' Party, 25
Solanas, Javier, 97–98
Solé, Robert, 28
South Africa, 212–13
Soviet Union. See Union of Soviet Socialist Republics
Spain: Arab tutelage of, 31; Madrid, March 11 terrorist attacks in, 15; Morocco, dispute with, 97
Spinoza, Baruch, 106
Stalin, Josef, 14
Steiner, George, 199

Stendhal. *See* Beyle, Marie-Henri

Stora, Benjamin, 7, 124n, 172

Sultan, Wafa, 47

Switzerland, 206

terrorism/terrorists: as an enemy,
re-evaluations of principles
and beliefs forced by, 137–38;
certainty of, incompatibility
of freedom/democracy and,
38–39; European reactions to
attacks, 14–22; tolerance for
Palestinian, 76–77

Third Worldism, 11–13, 132–33.
See also anti-Occidentalism

Thousand and One Nights, 159

Thucydides, 138

Thuram, Lilian, 163

Tocqueville, Alexis de, 91, 109,
204

trials and litigation: as the locus
of all struggles, 146–48; new
approach to the political metaphor of, 220–21

Tribu K, 150n

Trotsky, Leon, 154

Truman, Harry, 103

Truth and Reconciliation Commission (South Africa), 212

Tunisia, 155

Turkey, 37n

Tutu, Desmond, 212

Union of Soviet Socialist Republics (USSR), 13–14

United Nations (UN), resolution
condemning Zionism, 63

United States: Bush administration deviations from
American norms, dangers
and recovery from, 207–11; as
chief menace to world peace,
perception of, 65n; cult of
possibility and religion of
the future, devotion to, 96;
democracy and violence in,
72–73; democracy as political
religion in, 88–89; errors and
atonement for, dynamism of,
90–92; Europe and, comparisons and contrasts between
(*See* Old and New Worlds);
failure to act during 1994
genocide, apology for, 41n;
Israel and, 64n; the Obama
administration, new ap-
proach by, 223–25; oppressed
peoples, as best avenue of ap-
peal for, 98; as a "rogue state,"
21–22; September 11 terrorist
attacks against, 14; shifting
the blame to, 58; slavery,
sacrifice in the Civil War
to abolish, 155

USSR. *See* Union of Soviet Socialist Republics

Valéry, Paul, 171, 193

Vatican II Council, 44

Vattimo, Gianni, 34–35n, 199

victims and victimization: as
a career, 140–48; hereditary
transmission of status of,
99; hierarchy of martyrol-

ogy, Hitlerizing history and, 126–27; memory and, 157–63; reconciliation, 212–14; as a second servitude, 152–54; the Shoah as feeding a perverse metaphysics of, 114–17

Vidal-Naquet, Pierre, 123n

Villepin, Dominique de, 18–19, 201–2

Voltaire. *See* Arouet, Françoise-Marie

von Trotha, Adrian Dietrich Lothar, 123

Wilde, Oscar, 57

Wilkomirski, Binjamin, 114n.2

Woolf, Virginia, 27

Yemen, 155

Yudhoyono, Susilo Bambang, 52n

Zapatero, José Luis Rodríguez, 15, 18

Zero, Karl, 78

Zionism: Nazism and, parallel drawn between, 67–71; villifying of, 63–67. *See also* Israel

Zweig, Stefan, 73